Single: Living Your Own Way

Single

Living Your Own Way

by Buff Bradley, Jan Berman, Murray Suid, Roberta Suid

 Addison-Wesley Publishing Company
Reading, Massachusetts • Menlo Park, California
London • Amsterdam • Don Mills, Ontario • Sydney

Library of Congress Cataloging in Publication Data

Main entry under title:

Single.

    1. Single people. I. Bradley, Buff, 1943-
HQ800.S53   301.42'72'0652   77-8l633
ISBN 0-201-07477-X
ISBN 0-201-07476-1 pbk.

Third printing, November 1977

Illustrated by Jane Kiskaddon

Designed by Mike Shenon

ISBN 0-201-07476-1-P
ISBN 0-201-07477-X-H
ABCDEFGHIJ-AL-7987

For Theo Jung

Text Acknowledgements

Addison-Wesley Publishing Company: Excerpt from *Shyness* by Philip Zimbardo. Copyright © 1977 by Philip Zimbardo, Inc. Reprinted by permission of Addison-Wesley Publishing Company.

Crown Publishers, Inc.: Excerpt from *The Joy of Sex* by Alex Comfort, M.D., Ph.D. Copyright © 1972 by Mitchell Beazley Publishers Limited. Used by permission of Crown Publishers, Inc.

Dialogue House Library: Excerpt from *At a Journal Workshop* by Ira Progoff. Copyright © 1975 by Ira Progoff. Reprinted by permission of Dialogue House Library.

Doubleday & Company, Inc.: Excerpt from *Sylvia Porter's Money Book* by Sylvia Porter. Copyright © 1975 by Sylvia Porter. Reprinted by permission of Doubleday & Company, Inc., and Brandt & Brandt.

Farrar, Straus & Giroux, Inc.: Excerpt from *The Vagabond* by Colette, translated by Enid McLeod. Copyright © 1955 by Farrar, Straus & Young (now Farrar, Straus & Giroux, Inc.). Reprinted by permission of Farrar, Straus & Giroux, Inc., and Martin Secker & Warburg Ltd.

Harcourt, Brace and Jovanovich, Inc.: Excerpt from *Peg Bracken's Appendix to The I Hate to Cook Book* by Peg Bracken. Copyright © 1966 by Peg Bracken. Reprinted by permission of Harcourt, Brace and Jovanovich, Inc., and Arlington Books Ltd.

Alfred A. Knopf, Inc.: Excerpt from *The Odd Woman* by Gail Godwin. Copyright © 1974 by Gail Godwin. Reprinted by permission of Alfred A. Knopf, Inc., and Jonathan Cape, Ltd.

Little, Brown and Company: Excerpt from *The Book of Eve* by Constance Beresford-Howe. Copyright © 1973 by Constance Beresford-Howe. Reprinted by permission of Little, Brown and Company and The Macmillan Company of Canada Limited.

Macmillan Publishing Co., Inc.: Excerpt from *The Art of Eating* by M.F.K. Fisher. Copyright © 1937, 1941, 1942, 1943, 1948, 1949, 1954 by M.F.K. Fisher. Copyrights renewed 1971, 1976, 1977 by Mary Kennedy Friede (M.F.K. Fisher). Reprinted by permission of Macmillan Publishing Co., Inc., and Russell & Volkening, Inc.

William Morrow & Company, Inc.: Excerpt from *Widow* by Lynn Caine. Copyright © 1974 by Lynn Caine. Reprinted by permission of William Morrow

Mynabird Publishing: Excerpt from *Eat Alone With Your Children and Like It* by Susan Minard and Paula M. Berka. Copyright © 1976 by Mynabird Publishing. Reprinted by permission of Mynabird Publishing.

The New York Times: Excerpt from "How to Spend a Weekend Alone" by Joyce Maynard in the November 26, 1976 issue. Copyright © 1976 by The New York Times Company. Reprinted by permission of The New York Times Company.

W.W. Norton & Company, Inc.: Excerpt from *Plant Dreaming Deep* by May Sarton. Copyright © 1968 by May Sarton. Reprinted by permission of W.W. Norton & Company, Inc., and Russell & Volkening, Inc.

Prentice-Hall, Inc.: Excerpt from *Single* by Peter J. Stein. Copyright © 1976 by Peter J. Stein. Reprinted by permission of Prentice-Hall, Inc.

Prentice-Hall, Inc.: Excerpt from *The New Communes: Coming Together in America* by Ron E. Roberts. Copyright © 1971 by Ron E. Roberts. Reprinted by permission of Prentice-Hall, Inc.

St. Martin's Press, Inc.: Excerpt from *Survival Guide for the Suddenly Single* by Barbara Berson and Ben Bova. Copyright © 1974 by Barbara Berson and Ben Bova. Reprinted by permission of St. Martin's Press, Inc.

Charles Scribner's Sons: Excerpt from *The Last of the Mountain Men* by Harold Peterson. Copyright © 1969 by Harold Peterson. Reprinted by permission of Charles Scribner's Sons.

Simon & Schuster: Excerpt from *Lonely in America* by Suzanne Gordon. Copyright © 1976 by Suzanne Gordon. Reprinted by permission of Simon & Schuster, a Division of Gulf & Western Corporation.

Stein and Day Publishers: Excerpt from *The Pleasure Book* by Julius Fast. Copyright © 1975 by Julius Fast. Reprinted by permission of Stein and Day Publishers.

Ten Speed Press: Excerpt from *What Color is Your Parachute?* by Richard Nelson Bolles. Copyright © 1972 by Richard Nelson Bolles. Reprinted by permission of Ten Speed Press.

Table of Contents

Introduction

This book is about what it's like to be single in a predominantly couple society. It is meant to be a useful book for people who are single now and for those who may become single in the future. The text presents ways of coping with the recurrent problems of being single; suggests resources for living single-handedly; and, perhaps most important, celebrates the often overlooked joys of singleness.

The heart of the book is the testimony of the experts. Now there are experts and there are experts. The real experts, to our way of thinking, are those who experience the issues of single living every day, not the ones who peek and poke at singles with scientific instruments, statistical studies, and sociological analyses. The real experts are single people themselves. Thus, in the pages that follow, dozens of single people speak in their own voices about their own lives.

In preparing the book we conducted numerous tape-recorded interviews and also sent questionnaires to people throughout the country. This approach raised an important question at the start: Who is single? Unlike marriage, singleness isn't an easy state to define. We don't have single licenses. Divorce decrees notwithstanding, there are no singling ceremonies in which one person stands before an official promising to love, honor, and obey him- or herself.

At what point does a young person become single? Is it at 18 or 21? Or upon leaving the parental home? Is a person single if he or she lives alone but has one steady, long-term romantic relationship? How about someone who lives with a partner but is not married?

While some writers have put forth rather stringent criteria for qualifying as a single, we decided to take the opposite tack, to include as many of the various states of singleness as we could find. We interviewed people who had been single their entire lives, and others just recently "single again" following divorce or bereavement. We interviewed people who live by themselves, and others who live with their children, with roommates, or with large communal groups. Some of the interviewees are glad to be single. Others would rather be in a couple situation. We even talked with a woman who is happily married but living apart from her husband in her own house.

In a word, we were looking for diversity and we think we found it. Our respondents range in age from 24 to 73. They come from many parts of the country. They earn from $2000 to $40,000 a year. They are all essentially middle class, but they represent a myriad of attitudes, goals, and expectations. What they had in common was a willingness to share their lives and a desire to learn how others live.

One single woman told us she'd like to read a book on singles to find out if "other people are doing the same things I am or having the same thoughts." That's just what we hope the "folk wisdom" will do—provide points of reference and common experiences, so any single person who reads it may feel a little less isolated.

(Non-singles, we should add, may also find this material valuable. Singles clearly have much to teach about such important issues as identity, aloneness, solitude, friendship, and love. And, finally, it is a hard fact that many, many married people will be single again at some time in their lives, through the death of their mate or through divorce. This "folk wisdom'' can help people pay attention to that possibility and even prepare for it.)

The book is divided into three sections. Part I—Stories—contains 11 in-depth accounts of living the single life. None of the storytellers considers himself or herself a model of how to be a single parent, a bachelor, a widow, or whatever. Yet taken together these personal tales give a real sense of what it's like to be single at this time.

Part II—Skills—focuses on everyday situations. Here, singles talk about everything from cooking, household chores, and health to friendship, sex, and solitude. Each comment is tagged with a pseudonym plus the person's age. If the person was formerly married, we provide data on his or her current status—e.g., how long divorced. If no such marital information appears, then that person has always been single.

While certain strong themes emerge—for instance, the importance of friendship, the pride of self-sufficiency—there is a mind-boggling lack of consensus on almost every topic. We found as much diversity about what to do with dinner leftovers as leftover lovers. One person talks about the pleasure of seeing a movie alone; someone else considers that to be a torture. We gathered a catalogue of remedies for loneliness—from sleep to drink to mental gymnastics. But one woman says she welcomes loneliness as an emotion worth feeling. The voices demonstrate that there are an incredible number of life styles that work.

To complement the "folk wisdom," this section also includes writings by Thoreau, Colette, Whitman, and others. In addition, there are some 70 reviews of books that address one or another of the key issues.

The final part of the book—Questions—contains the questionnaire we used in obtaining the stories and comments of single people.

You might use it as a way of taking stock of your own life.

While it's hard, as we've indicated, to pin down singleness with sociological precision, one thing is clear: There are a lot of single people in America today. The U.S. Census Bureau tells us there are 25 million adults who have never been married, six and a half million divorced persons, ten million widows, two million widowers, and three and a half million separated people.

The business world has taken note of the whopping size of the amorphous "singles market." The industry includes singles apartment complexes, singles bars, singles travel agencies, and, of course, myriad dating services. Publishers also have recognized singles in a big way. A decade ago you'd have been hard put to find a handful of books dealing with the single state (other than those silly guides to finding dates and mates). Now there are dozens of serious books being published every year dealing with one or another aspect of singleness. And single people themselves are becoming ever more conscious about the problems and possibilities of their various life styles. This is what *Single: Living Your Own Way* is all about.

We began *Single: Living Your Own Way* thinking that single people's lives ought to be viewed more seriously and more positively. We finished convinced that single people in America are a vast and mostly untapped national resource, that they have much to tell and teach about what it means to live on one's own. And as more than one wise person has said, until we come to terms with the self alone, stripped of all accoutrements and relationships, we can't ever really know who we are.

Part I Stories

Lynn's Story

A 45-year-old executive leads an independent life.

Virtually all of my friends married within two or three years of graduation from college. Now, when you think about that, it's weird. Here we were—highly educated women. Many of us went to graduate school. Our families expected us to be well-educated. But, at the same time, they expected us to marry. Somehow education made you a good adjunct to your husband. Or it was something you could use "in case something happened to your husband." But all this was dependent on your marrying. For the most part you weren't expected to be a person in your own right, really. I can remember discussing with my friends the fact that we wanted somebody who could "dominate us." Which now seems to be a terribly silly, outmoded concept if it ever had any validity.

I was under this family pressure and the pressure of the times. And I must say that when I was in my 20s I thought I wanted to marry. On the most conscious level I thought that was what I wanted to do. As a result, I suffered quite a bit from not being married. I became neurotic about it actually. I went into therapy on the eve of my 30th birthday because that seemed like such a dreadful turning point.

So let's say I thought I wanted to get married when I was in my 20s. Now, with the perspective of 20 years, that is to say, now that I'm middle-aged, and also with the changing cultural perspective, I look back and I realize that unconsciously I didn't want to marry. Had the real me wanted to marry, I would have done so. I went out a lot. I met a lot of people. I had a very active social life. I had a fairly active sex life, too. If you want to marry, you can marry. There are plenty of people around wanting to get married. I look back and I say, really, I didn't want to marry or I would have done so.

So now the question is, Why didn't I want to marry? The answer is complex. I had a very strong, very dominating father. My mother and father had a good marriage. They were married for 55 years and it worked. They had four children. They respected each other. I think they loved each other. But my mother lived a very traditional existence as a submissive wife. Not that she was a little mouse or anything. But it never occurred to her to work or to express herself as an individual too much.

I was born a fairly independent individual, assertive and wanting my own way. I can remember when I was very small, I think probably four years old, I used to play a little game in which I was *boss of the world*. Those were my words. And I think, as I look back on it, that I must have gotten the idea very early on that I didn't want anyone pushing me around, especially someone like the only real male role model in my life, my father. He liked power. He liked money. He liked influence.

So this independence got into me very early on. It deepened as I grew into my teens and 20s, unconsciously again, always with the social pressure overlaying it. But it apparently was deep enough so that I didn't ever get married. It's conceivable that with the changing times and my growth and possibly the growth of the men around me, that I could marry in my 50s or 60s. People do it.

When I was about 35 years old, I began to think consciously, "I'm not going to get married." At that point several big changes occurred in my life. I moved across

Boss of the World

the country away from my family and that lessened their influence. A while later my mother died. When you lose a parent it's a real break in your life, lots of things shift. A brake is off you. That is to say, your parents have certain expectations of you and as long as they're alive you try, to some extent, to live up to their standards.

Shortly after my mother died I had an affair with a woman. That was a huge break. The idea of having an affair with a woman never occurred to me when I was in my 20s. That made me think that maybe one of the reasons why I hadn't married was because I had some deeply rooted sexual hang-ups, my feelings about my father or something. I don't know, because I still was attracted to men. But it made me think that perhaps I had a little bit of hostility towards men that I hadn't realized. It didn't make me think that I was a "lesbian." That's not a word that I like at all because it labels a person so that's all you think about her. As if she had nothing in her life but sex, right? I just don't like the word at all.

Being single is only one fact of my life.
And I don't think it has enough substance to
constitute joining a club for.

I had roommates pretty much through my 20s. It was partly financial, partly because that was just what was done. You shared with other girls when you were right out of college. I had a house with three other girls once. And we had a lot of fun.

I started living all alone about 12 or 13 years ago. My roommate left and there I was. I could afford to maintain the apartment on my own. Then, when I moved to a new state, I didn't know anyone to share with and I think that as you get older and you have more money, you prize your privacy a little bit more. I live alone and I enjoy it.

I like privacy and the independence and the fact that it's my place. I can run it the way I want it. You don't have to compromise all the time about differences in the way things are done. But of course, nothing is perfect. It would be very nice to have someone to share dinner with every night. And sharing other things, breakfast or a good television program or whatever. But for the most part I like it this way.

Back in the 1960s, it never occurred to me that I, a single woman, could ever own a house. Finally it began to creep up on me that I had as much right as anyone else to own a house. It took a long time. I can remember a friend once saying, "Well, you'll probably buy yourself a house some time." And I can remember saying,"Oh, everyone would think I was that eccentric single woman on the block." I had been renting apartments always. But when it hit me it hit me with a force, that I had every right to own a house. I could afford it so I bought one. It's a real home and a hobby with me, maintaining it and having it be attractive. I really enjoy all the household chores.

I do quite a bit of entertaining. I invite someone for dinner once or twice a week. And I have parties. I'm giving a party for 50 people the week after next. I like to give parties. I'm a social person. I like social intercourse. My parents were both quite social; they entertained a lot. It was just part of their lives, making friends through entertaining and of course reciprocating when they were entertained. I have that same thing.

For years I was very strict about having equal numbers of men and women at my parties. That's just the way things were done. And I suppose it made me more comfortable. I've gotten over that now, though. I will invite couples, without having someone for myself. But I think that married couples are hesitant about entertaining single women without getting "someone" for them.

There are two married couples, friends of mine, who are very conventional, very well-off people, and they have a very active social life. They're constantly entertaining. But they don't entertain me very much unless it's a situation like Thanksgiving and they think I might be alone.

I can't identify their motives for not inviting me more often. It may be the women feel threatened to have a single woman around their husbands. And also that a lot of men of that generation get uncomfortable in the presence of single women. I think it's because they're afraid that the women are after them.

Traveling is something I really like to do—to go someplace out of the state and preferably out of the country. And I do like to travel with someone. That can be a little bit of a problem for me, for any single person I imagine, because

Now one is even sometimes admired for having been an independent woman, for having withstood the temptation of getting married.

you don't have a built-in traveling companion. You have to find someone with whom you're compatible. The people that you love are not always the people you can travel with. Living with someone or being around them is sometimes different from traveling with them. My best friend and I went to France a couple of years ago and we didn't travel very well together at all. We had different expectations and different rhythms and we had some quite serious differences, really, even though we get along wonderfully at home.

I have found that my sister and brother-in-law and I are wonderful as traveling companions. It's great when you're single to find people you can travel with. We've been to Mexico together and this year we're going to do England. I've never taken a package tour but I wouldn't mind doing it, depending on the situation. I wouldn't mind because I'd have a reasonable expectation of having something in common with the other people.

I really like meeting people in some context, whether it be work or school or some enterprise that I happen to be working on. I worked for a couple of years on a volunteer project for the recreation department and really enjoyed my association with those people. They're still my friends.

I don't think it's very satisfactory to join a singles group just because one is single. That word "single"—I feel the same way about it as I do about the word "lesbian." Being single is only one fact of my life. And I don't think it has enough substance to constitute joining a club for. Now, I play bridge, for instance, and I enjoy playing bridge in community situations but that has some substance to it. You're there for a reason.

Night school or college courses are like

that, too. They have a substance, there's the content of the courses, and you might meet people with whom you had something in common through a course. But to go to one of these singles clubs doesn't appeal to me.

As I said earlier, I have not categorically ruled out the possibility of marriage. I have certain qualifications. For example, ideally, I'd like to live in a big place so that I wouldn't be on top of this person. Someone was telling me the other day about a marriage he knew of where the partners lived in two different cities and they only saw each other half of the week or every other week or something like that. And I said that that would probably be very satisfactory for me. Having lived my entire adult life without a mate, I imagine the adjustment would be quite something.

But I'm not actively seeking a mate. And it wouldn't do me much good if I was. After all, there aren't that many men of the appropriate age available at this time. They're all going out with young chicks. Or they're still married. Or they're gay.

I am much more comfortable personally about my single state today than I was 15 years ago because of my own growth and personal circumstances. And also because the single state is not only more accepted, but in some cases even admired now. Twenty years ago it was anathema, not to mention 50 years ago—the stigma of the old maid, the spinster. Those images were very, very entrenched. And I think that that has changed. Now, one is even sometimes admired for having been an independent woman for quite a long time, for having withstood the temptations of getting married.

Bruce's Story

A 38-year-old divorced father develops his skills as a single parent.

The most immediate problem that I faced when my wife left was learning to feel good about myself in the situation, learning to think that I could cope with the whole process of being alone. That was the hardest part for me to go through. The next problem was learning how to take care of the children—my ten-year-old son and my eight-year-old daughter.

Initially, I didn't do very well at being alone. I sought the help of a psychotherapist. At the time the separation occurred I was in the middle of a huge project at work. I was putting in an enormous amount of time. There was a deadline I had to meet. It became impossible for me to worry about my emotional problems at one place and worry about my work problems at another place. I couldn't sort them out. I'd be at work and I'd be worrying about my emotional problems and my family life. And then I'd be at home and I'd be worrying about my work problems. So, in an attempt to separate those two domains, I went to a psychotherapist and that really turned the trick. He helped me to see a lot of things that were going on and how I was reacting to them.

The first time I saw the therapist I broke down and cried and did the whole bit. I was a little embarrassed about that. But as I look back on it now it was the proper thing to do. It gave him the best perspective, the best information in the shortest amount of time to see where I was emotionally. Had I held back and not done that it might have taken weeks or months longer for him to see where I was. And it was useful. It got a lot of stuff out of me.

The therapist didn't solve my problems, but he allowed me to get them all out in the open so I could consciously think about my emotions. You can see what's going on, look at it and determine where you are, and then take some action rather than just wallow in indecision. I think I could have figured it out without therapy, but it would have taken longer. I started seeing the therapist in May and by September I felt really good. By September, all the decisions had been made about separation and living arrangements and custody of the children.

At first, there was no battle over the kids. My ex-wife left because she wanted to be with her boy friend. Not having kids around was an advantage for that relationship.

I told her that I wanted the children and I was going to stay in the house. She agreed and she got a little apartment. Since then I think her relationship with that man has waned, although I'm not sure. I think she's felt a stronger need for the children and has felt like I was taking them away from her. I have since been to court four or five times on the custody issue and have spent a lot of money to retain custody of them.

The children were very upset by it all. They obviously did not want to have to decide where to go. There were some real terror scenes involving the children—physical struggles at the door, that kind of thing. And they've suffered because of that.

At the same time, I was swamped with day-to-day concerns. How do I provide for these children? How do I find baby-sitters? How do I cook meals? How do I wash clothes? I had some domestic skills but it was overpowering, having all these things to do at one time, making sure I could get to the grocery store, taking care of the house, getting them off to school, baby-sitting after school.

Initially, my former wife did some baby-sitting at the house with the children. As the situation wore on it became clear that I was suffering because of that. I had a lot of resentment. I was finally getting a hold of what our relationship was and how I felt I had been manipulated by her. I resented her being there with the children, and I finally ended that arrangement.

I decided to hire a full-time baby-sitter after school. I placed an advertisement in the paper. I had 15 inquiries and I had 10 interviews. I just fumbled through it. I had a list of points that I wanted to tell them about—my schedule and what I expected of them and things like that. Then there were questions I asked them—what experience they had, what their situation was, did they have a car. I looked at it as just an employer-employee relationship—what's important and what do people expect, getting everything up front as much as possible. I tried to put myself in the employee's situation: When's this guy going to be here? What does he want me to do?

Last summer my former wife, without warning, moved back into the house.

The woman I hired interacted well with the kids during the interview. I asked the children, "Which one did you like?" And they said they liked this particular woman. She showed interest in them. She showed interest in me. She showed interest in the situation. We had tea and we talked for a long time. One of the strong impressions I got was that she's going to be happy doing the job; she's not going to go off tomorrow looking for another job. She works part-time for an insurance company in the mornings and she gets off at three and stays here every afternoon until I come home.

Most of the housework I do myself. The first year I was separated I spent a lot of time doing it and I really felt overworked. There were a lot of things I didn't get done that I wanted to get done. I just did the basics. I got all the clothes washed. I got all the dishes washed. I got the sheets changed once a week. But the house was generally dirty. The cobwebs didn't get swept out and the utility room didn't get swept out; the floors didn't get waxed. The windows didn't get washed. Things like that.

This year I've decided it's worth some money having somebody do all that, so my baby-sitter is responsible for at least getting the dishes done. If I don't get my bed made up in the morning, she makes it. Some days I ask her specifically to clean the bathroom or vacuum all the rugs or whatever. She takes a lot of pressure off so that when I get home I don't have to wash a thousand dishes or pots and pans before I can even start dinner.

This summer, when the children were spending about three weeks with their mother, I found myself doing the things that I couldn't ordinarily do like waxing the floors and washing windows.

Cooking is something I like to do. Before, I had a few things that I could cook really well, but I could not do short-order cooking at all. And I wasn't imaginative about what went with what. I still don't have a very good feel for spices and things like that, but I do have a much better idea of what things can go together and how to do it quickly.

I learned by doing. And I read. I started reading cookbooks. Now I find myself really liking to look at cookbooks. I go to a bookstore and the first place I go is to the cookbook section. I use different things from different cookbooks. I have just recently started using the *Tassajara Bread Book*. I use *Diet for a Small Planet* and *Recipes for a Small Planet*. *Joy of Cooking* is for very basic stuff like how to poach or how to boil.

The technical household problems were solved relatively easily. I had more trouble figuring out where the children were emotionally with the dissolution and where they were emotionally at school and what they needed. I was trying to straighten out my own head and figure out where I was in addition to worrying about where they were too. I tried to get my own head squared away first. There was about a four-month's period in which I didn't worry about them very much, in the sense of their emotional needs. They were just there, kind of hanging on.

Now, I really listen to them. I listen not only to what they say but what their feelings are. And I tell them what my feelings are too.

I feel good that I can really function by myself and have a household and raise two children.

I'm not afraid to be angry at them. In the relationship with my former wife no anger was allowed at all. You couldn't shout at anybody. You couldn't be angry. You couldn't be hostile. And so all those feelings got repressed. That was her way.

Now it's a whole different ball game. Here's a kid who's done something I don't want him to do. My ex-wife's not around telling me how to handle it. So I finally get to the point of saying, "You know, I really am angry at you, damn it." Then he reacts and tells me he's angry. All right, everybody knows everybody's angry and that's O.K. I think they understand that now. I don't think they did before. I certainly didn't understand it, particularly with the children.

I know my kids now. I don't feel like I really knew them before. They were little people in the house and they had certain kinds of needs. I provided mostly for their material needs but not very much for their emotional needs. We did a lot of things together but we didn't do much emotional stuff together.

Now we do. And my son has turned into a fantastic person as far as I'm concerned. My daughter and I still battle a lot. But my son and I are really drawing close together. I think it's very necessary at this stage in his development for him to feel like that. I think that's going to come a little bit later for my daughter. She's two years younger than he is.

I think they're doing well. That's the feedback that I get from them and also from their school. They see my psychotherapist occasionally, maybe once every two months. I have a very good feeling about where they are now.

The kids like to go see their mother. That's no problem. I think she satisfies certain needs for them and I think they should see her. My daughter, particularly, needs some sort of a female image occasionally to relate to. Their mother and I tend to complement each other in what we give them. I have certain things I want to give them and I'm sure she has certain things that she wants to share with them. She sees them every other weekend, from Friday night until Sunday evening, and spends two evenings a week at dinner with them.

Things right now are fairly calm between all of us—the kids, my former wife, and me. But it hasn't always been that way. Last summer my former wife, without warning, moved back into the house. She appeared one Friday afternoon. I called the police. But my attorney had to get a court order to get her out. Then he took off for a vacation and she got a counter-order and moved back in. She stayed there for three of the tensest weeks of my life. The children became very confused about why she was there, wondering if she was going to stay there. This was a year after she had left.

That's when the custody problems started. I think she thought it would help her custody case if she were living in the house. It did just the opposite. The social worker came and saw the children and clearly saw what was going on. And so when we went to court there was evidence to say that that should have never happened.

I still have dreams about that. I had a dream the other night that she moved back in the house again. It was so powerful that I wanted to get out of bed and go look to make sure that she wasn't there. That's how much it really upset me. It was just total insanity as far as I was concerned.

I'm more aware of
myself as a person than
I ever was before.

I don't want to have anything to do with her now. What she does with the children is her life. What I do with the children is my life. She picks the kids up in the evenings and I just choose not to be here. I work late. The baby-sitter stays until she comes. It's got to the point where there's nothing to say to my ex-wife. I'm not going to stand at the door and argue with her about anything.

We communicate mostly through lawyers. It's a very expensive way of communication. In fact, I have a lot of debts now. I hope that sooner or later we can talk to each other directly, but emotionally it just doesn't seem possible right now. For me, she's somebody that I don't want in my life any more and the less I have to do with her, the better off I am. I don't know how long it will take before I can just let the hostility go.

There was a period right after the separation of proving myself, of having a lot of sex with different women, making sure that the breakup wasn't due to that. That was pretty satisfying in a very physical sense. Emotionally, it wasn't very satisfying. And then, of course, you go through that stage, you prove what you need to prove, and then it just kind of mellows out from there.

I don't have quickies or one-night stands. I like being with people I enjoy, people I've known for a while. I've been to a couple of dating bars but I've found that you have to go with the right expectations. I've been able to do that a couple of times and a couple of times I haven't. Overall, I have found that's not the best way, so I just don't do it any more. A friend of mine said it's usually feast or famine. And right now is a famine.

My daughter gives me occasional feedback about dating. I can remember very precisely one evening she came to me after I had had a woman friend over for dinner and she said, "You know, Dad, it sure is nice to have a woman here." She really enjoys having another woman around the house once in a while. It doesn't matter much to my son. It doesn't bother him one way or the other.

I have no plans whatsoever to get into any kind of a permanent situation. But that might change. For now I don't think I'm capable of it, or even desire to have a permanent relationship. I don't want to be tied down. I feel good that I can really function by myself and have a household and raise two children.

It used to depress me to think I might always be single. It doesn't particularly now. The visions that came up, the fantasies I had, were of this little old dried up man who has nobody. But I think you make that for yourself. If that's what you want for yourself, that's what you'll be. And if you decide to be something else, you'll be something else. You don't have to be that. Even if you are an old man alone by yourself, you can still be happy.

You don't have to be unhappy about your situation. I learned that, I think, when I began feeling good about myself and my own capabilities, really coming to grips with the fact that I determine my own destiny. Nobody else out there does it. I'm the one who has to do it for myself. And if I decide I want something different, I have to make it happen.

I'm more aware of myself as a person than I ever was before. As I look back on it, on my married life, I can see now that I was really dying as an individual, and at some point I would have crashed into the ground and burned.

Adele's Story

A 59-year-old widow discovers a new life.

During the last eight years of my husband's life he stopped wanting to grow. After his retirement he liked to spend the whole morning just reading the paper and lolling around. I resented the fact that because he had retired he thought that I had to retire too. I still wanted to dance. I was jogging. I was playing tennis. I was eager to do all sorts of things. He said he thought I was being silly, acting that way at my age. But I didn't want him to define me. That's something I've never let anyone do.

After Martin died, a year ago, there were some couples who wanted to swallow me up and have me become an integral part of their lives. I pushed them aside because that wasn't for me. I told them, "I'm not going to become a little old lady sitting in your living room who's always there when everybody comes over." I loved being at their Easter egg hunts and various family events. But that wasn't taking care of me when I was lonely and in bed alone. I told them, "I love you dearly but you're not the beginning and the end of the rest of my life."

I'm not saying that I did without help when my husband died. I needed friends desperately. I had a lot of grief and it was mixed with some guilt because near the end I was just hoping he would go. I had been his custodian for a long time. And he no longer looked anything like the man I had married and loved. He hated the way he looked. It was so sad. I hated to see him despise his looks. I hated to see him suffer.

I thought I was prepared for his death. Yet when it actually came I didn't know which way to turn. We had been together 31 years. We had shared an enormous number of adventures. We had raised a family. When the burden of caring for him was gone, the loneliness was overwhelming. I found myself needing somebody to stay with me. I couldn't bear being alone. So I had a series of friends come and spend the night with me.

At first, everything I tried to do took a lot of conscious effort. I wanted to keep busy but nothing came spontaneously. It took about six months until I got past that part of the mourning period, until I was able to plan my day, do my laundry, read a book, arrange flowers without it taking an extraordinary act of will.

Making new friends has helped. A lot of my old couple friends are dropping away now. The wife of one of them says her husband has trouble seeing me because whenever we're together all he thinks about is my husband. So I know that that relationship is going to collapse. But I don't think that's so terrible. I look back when my husband was alive. We had a lot of women friends who became widows and we didn't go to a hell of a lot of trouble to see them after their husbands died. In all honesty, we didn't. We didn't blacklist consciously. But we just didn't invite them over very often.

So this is happening to me now and it forces me to find fresh faces. I recently met a couple at a party. They never knew Martin. The three of us had an immediate rapport. We've become very close friends. They take me out as if I were a couple. They find me great fun to be with. Just me! And that makes me feel terrific about myself.

Relationships with men have been very important to me. It has been a pleasant surprise to discover in the past few months that several 35- to 40-year-old men have been attracted to me. Of course, I lie like hell about how old I am, if they ever ask.

But most of them are discrete enough just to ignore the whole subject of age. After all, I'm almost 60.

Anyway, I'm keeping a little notebook on my sexual encounters because I keep forgetting who's who. I write down their names and give them a little editorial—whether they were good or bad or indifferent.

My most fantastic experience happened during a trip abroad. An old French couple who had been friends of ours invited me to lunch. They chose an interesting out-of-the-

way restaurant that is only open for lunch. You need reservations two weeks in advance. It's one of those old-fashioned marvelous places—very bistro-like so that everybody sits very close to everybody else. At the table next to ours, very close, were two men. One older man and a young man. The young man was facing in my direction and I was aware that he was looking at me. Every time I'd look up, his eye would catch mine, so I'd look away. But then I'd be drawn back to him. And suddenly he asked the waiter for some scrap paper. He

I thought I was prepared for his death.
Yet when it actually came
I didn't know which way to turn.

was trying to write something down for his friend. And the waiter went into the kitchen and came out with an enormous roll, about a yard long, of brown butcher paper. It was tremendous. Everybody in the restaurant started to laugh. He could have written a book on that piece of paper. Well, I had a pad with me and I quickly tore some sheets off and handed them to him.

A little while later he tapped my friend on the shoulder and said, "The lady gave me more sheets than I need." All this in French. He could hear me speak in French to my friend, but with my American accent. Undoubtedly he recognized it. So my friend handed the sheets back to me and I could see that there was a note on one of them. It started off in English and ended in French. And the note simply said, "You're beautiful. I must see you. This is my phone number, and my name. Please call me." After that, I could not look at him.

We left the restaurant about 2:30 and all day I was looking at that piece of paper and saying, "Should I? Shouldn't I? Should I? Shouldn't I?" Finally, at 5:30, I called and left a message. He called me back that evening and he said, "All day I've been wondering, Will she? Won't she? Will she? Won't she?" And he spoke perfect English. He was an Italian from Turino.

Three or four nights later we finally got together. When he came to pick me up I knew, I just knew, that I was going to go to bed with him. And he knew too. There was no question about it. But the way it happened was nice because he planned dinner at this wonderful restaurant. We had to travel 45 minutes to get to it. He sat opposite me and he did something that had never been done to me before which was nice, because at my age I thought every-

thing had been done to me. He took a shoe off and he put his toe up between my legs. And I thought, "Oh, my God, I'll never be able to leave this restaurant." We were having coffee and brandy and his foot's up there. Finally he said, "Are we going back to your place?" I said, "That's impossible. My friends would never countenance such a thing." "Well," he said, "my hotel." I said, "I won't go to a hotel."

So there we were. Then he said, "Well, my office."

"Fine," I said.

We went to his office. I'm not sure why I wouldn't go to his hotel. I guess because I once stayed in that hotel with Martin and I just didn't want to do it. We went to his office and there was a refrigerator there filled with champagne. There were no couches or anything. But there was a rug on the floor and we decided that that was going to be fine. He brought the champagne out and at one point in the evening he poured champagne all over my body and licked it off. It was lovely. And I thought, "Well, that's never happened to me either."

I had a very good time with him. It was just as natural as could be. He took all my phone numbers in Italy and Paris. When I came back to Paris after Italy he didn't call. I was so upset. I said, "Ah ha. He noticed how old I was. How stupid I was to allow myself to be so vulnerable. Why did I do that?" It made me feel so degraded.

But when I got back to the U.S. there was a letter from him in which he said, "I called and they said you had just left. I was delayed in London." I was so thrilled to get his letter, thrilled that he wanted to see me some more. He wanted me to come back for Christmas. I suppose he thinks I'm made of money.

I'm keeping a little notebook on my sexual encounters because I keep forgetting who's who.

The sex I have with all these young men is something that tells me I'm still desirable. Although I don't walk around thinking that I'm 59, the fact is I am, and there isn't much hope that I will find a relationship as easily as a woman who's in her 30s. I realize that I'm much closer to that period in my life when having a companion will be terribly, terribly important. The alternative to that will be going into a nursing home or a retirement village or something in order to have friends around me. I'm thinking in terms of the fact that even if I bear my age well, I'm still going to slow down when I get to 70, which is only 11 years away. Of course, you can do a lot of living in 11 years, but still, I think about that. I definitely don't want marriage. But I certainly would like the gentle companionship of a nice man. Someone to share things with. I really adore people with humor. That is one of the only things Martin didn't have a lot of. He wasn't a natural wit. And I find myself very attracted to men who are witty. It makes life so pleasant. And it doesn't mean that we won't be sexually active. Because I have friends in their 70s who are telling me that they are.

But there is so much more to a relationship than having sex. My husband and I were very social. There were dinners and being invited and inviting people back, and the stimulation of arranging the right people with the right people, and having parties that caused people to rave the next day and send all kinds of goodies because they had such a great time.

I love putting people together. I like mixing everybody up. That's something I can still do as a single woman but I don't have the same inclination to do it. It's a lot of hard work and when it's all over I'm alone. I don't have anybody to discuss it with, and that's such fun.

Actually, I'm hoping in some schoolgirlish way that the next man in my life, the next long relationship, will be a man very different from Martin, because I think it would be fun to try new things. I'd like a man whose head is screwed on in another way. When I meet him I'll know. But I wouldn't like to go back to the same well and to the same mold and find another Martin. I feel certain I'll find someone. I shouldn't feel that, I guess, because I have friends who are very attractive and have been alone for years. But somehow I think, in all honesty and without being snotty, I must have a little more zip than they have.

But I don't put all, or even most, of my energy into finding a man. The biggest thing in my life right now is a new job I got. It gives me much more purpose.

I'm the director of marketing for a new chain of retail shops. I was really nervous when I interviewed for the job although I've held executive positions other times in my life. But before I got this new job I knew I was spinning my wheels. I was making waves. I was keeping busy. But it was all meaningless. I needed a really challenging job. I needed to have some place to go to during the day, something that was interesting. Since I've started this job, I'm just ecstatic. Even meeting the girls in the office is fun. And trying to figure out solutions to hard problems. There's no way I could ever be lonely because the work fills me up. I find myself strolling around my office saying, "God, does everybody realize how happy I am?"

Tom's Story

A 30-year-old man wants to leave the single life behind.

When I turned 30 last spring it was a significant milestone. At this point in my life I would prefer to be married. I feel that as soon as I find someone I'm compatible with, I will get married.

I don't regret having been single all this time. It's been a really positive experience. I like the feeling of self-reliance. It's great not having to compromise my particular likes or dislikes. My refrigerator is filled with the kind of food I like to eat. I don't have to gain permission to be out with the boys; it's a total freedom.

What I don't like about being single is that it's very lonely to come home at five o'clock to an empty house. Actually, I'm a very social person and I have chosen to live with other people more times than not. I live alone right now, but I would prefer to have a roommate if there was someone I was compatible with. It just happens that I'm new to my job and the area, so I'm living alone.

When I'm living with a roommate I think of myself as a family member. So I'm very selective. I have to have somebody that is very neat, like I am, someone that has a very high level of sensitivity and is not afraid of being very open. I have to know the person pretty well ahead of time. For example, before I moved in with my last roommate, we played tennis and drank a lot of beer together to the point where we just knew that we had common feelings toward love and peace and all that kind of stuff. He and I became very much a family. We divvied up the assignments and we were pretty responsible for each other. It was a very good thing.

But now I'd rather be with a woman than have another male roommate. I'm getting to the point where I feel self-conscious at times about being 30 and not being married. It's acceptable to be single when you're in your 20s. Now I'm beginning to think maybe people are saying about me, "Is this person antisocial or what is wrong with this person?"

There's a lot of pressure to be part of a couple when you're a professional and 30 years old. People I work with tend to be married and so I'm just a minority, and each year that goes on I become more of a minority.

I honestly believe that it's just been a whole series of circumstances that's kept me from marrying. It's either been the right time in my life but not the woman's, or vice versa, for the past ten years. It's been a series of strange events that has caused me to be single at the age of 30.

Right now I'm in charge of the Christmas party and I'm wondering who the hell I'm going to take. That's because I have a real fear of showing up alone. Good God, I would prefer not to show up at all. But I have to because I'm running the whole thing. I'm sure I'll find someone.

In fact, a woman I went to college with ten years ago is now teaching near here and she and I talked about the fact that we would be happy to play dating service. If she goes to faculty parties or whatever and doesn't have a date, she'll call me up, and I will do the same. It's kind of like an insurance thing we have. There's nothing sexual, nothing romantic. It's just nice to have someone to do that with.

Naturally, I gravitate toward single people because we have similar interests. It's not as though I don't go to many parties attended by both groups. But there is definitely a kinship

of styles with singles.

Let's say a group from my office gets together after work on a Friday night and we go out and have a beer. The married people are all looking at their watches by about six o'clock. And I'm just ready for a second or third beer, and may end up going to dinner someplace or staying there another three hours and staggering home.

I've often lost intimate friends when they became married. And it's not that I'm not compatible and pleased with their spouses.

But it's just like they're going to another world. We may continue to be friends. But when they have a spouse, that puts a barrier into our relationship.

There are very few ways that single people meet other single people. At work, most of the people are paired off. I just can't see taking a psychology course at the extension school or joining the ski club for the explicit purpose of meeting someone. If I'm really interested in the subject

I'm getting to the point where I feel self-conscious at times about being 30 and not being married.

matter, fine. But I think that it can be a real waste of time to do that for the covert purpose of wanting to meet somebody.

I don't look for partners at dating bars any more. The last time I went to one was maybe three or four years ago. It is just such a superficial scene. The bar and disco scene is so sad. The ratio is usually about three males to every one female. I might ask a woman to dance and she'll say no. So I feel two feet tall and walk away and go back and have another belt. Then another man, who may be extremely handsome, asks her, and she'll say no to him. You know, I really do think some women get off on that.

I've had so many women tell me that they would never go to a place like that because the guys they would meet would be so plastic and the only thing they'd want would be to go to bed with them. But the times that I have gone I have sincerely wanted to meet a woman and could have cared less whether we went to bed that night or not. It's a lousy, lousy method for meeting people.

The most effective way I know to find women is through women friends, coaxing them to introduce me to their friends. A lot of them are hesitant to do that. "Well, I remember I fixed so-and-so up with a blind date and it was a real bomb." And I'll say, "But it really doesn't matter to me. I'm certainly not going to hold it against you if she's missing three teeth."

I just enjoy people. Maybe I'm different in that respect. I would never think that going out with someone for an evening could be anything but a good experience. Whether or not there was anything there for the future doesn't matter. I don't like to become a pest to people and say, "Hey, fix me up with your

friend." But I think that's the best technique so far. If I know something about Jane and Jane has a friend, then I can assume certain qualities about her friend.

The hard part is, the older I get, the more difficult it seems to be to meet women with whom I'm compatible. Maybe I'm being more selective. I think maybe that's a part of it. But, also, there seem to be fewer out there. Sometimes I just say, "Where the hell are all the women?"

There's been a big change in the last five or six years in women's attitudes. A hardness to them. Again, women I've been dating are older, certainly they've had more experiences with men than when I was 22. When I was 22, everything was fresh and young. But I'm certain that women's liberation is responsible for a lot of the changes. I look at it with the same kind of mournfulness I did when the mini-skirt went by the wayside. I think it's really too bad for both men and women. It's hard for males to interact with an educated woman. They're more certain about where they're at and yet they're really not. I think that dating is awkward for both males and females today.

I know very much the kind of woman that I'm looking for and feel that when I find her and if it's the right time in her life and we get married, it'll probably be a very successful marriage. That's just because I've gained so much from the hundreds of women I've gone out with and had relationships with.

Ideally, the woman I marry would be from a similar kind of class background, cultural background, middle-class, upper middle-class. She would have to be very sensitive and warm. I don't want to go on and on about it. I

I'm certain that by 40 I'll be married. I guess if I don't find the perfect woman I'll start dropping a few of the criteria.

think everybody looks for the same things.

I really need a woman who has her own stimulation and from whom I can gain some positive benefit from her interests. I could never marry a happy homebody who just wants to live and die for her husband's welfare. Probably the most important virtue that partners should have is respect.

It's crossed my mind that I may not find the right person and end up alone. But I'm certain that by 40 I'll be married. I guess if I don't find the perfect woman I'll start dropping a few of the criteria. I'll change my standards.

Weekends, in the meantime, are very depressing. Usually I try to have something to do. I'll go through every single resource I have. If I have nothing to do I will read a book or watch the tube or something like that. If this were six years ago I'd have no problem with going out alone to a singles bar.

I never go out to eat alone. That's too depressing, other than eating at a McDonald's. What I often do is pick up a hamburger someplace on my way home and then sit down in front of the TV set to eat dinner. I usually eat dinner with Walter Cronkite.

There have been nights when I've had a good appetite and thought, "Gee, it would really be great to try this Italian restaurant." But I just won't go in there because I would feel like a bump on a log. I would just feel very strange, sitting there all by myself. I wouldn't do it.

A healthy sex life is important to me. I usually know enough women so that even if we have nothing terribly romantic going at the time, we can have a sexually gratifying experience. The problem that frequently arises is that one of the two people tends to be more emotionally attached to the other. I've been on both sides of that. I would like to think that I could know a person and we could be good friends and have sex together and that's all. But I've never seen it work for any longer than a couple of months. And then one of the two people starts to freak out.

One thing that does concern me is that there is now, along with women's liberation and sexual liberation, a need for males to perform adequately. It is not uncommon to have sex with someone the first time you go out with her. A lot of times I perform very well. Other times I don't, because I feel like I'm on trial. How well am I going to do?

Many of my married friends seem to have something I don't. A very close friend of mine got married last spring and he and his wife, who are both professionals, just bought a home. Now I'm beginning to feel, "Hey, you know, you're not getting any younger and what do you have, a few thousand bucks in a savings account and a lot of potential." I'm beginning to feel it's really time that I started putting my house in order and stopped spending all this money on travel and other little things and started being more serious. It's O.K. when you're in your 20s, but I'm now 30 and here are my friends buying a beautiful home and really getting serious about life.

What I'm going through right now is almost this gentle panic about wanting to get married. Maybe I would be better as a single person for the rest of my life. But I don't believe that. I'm just tired of being single. It was great while it lasted but if I weigh both sides, I really choose to be married.

Jeff's Story

A 47-year-old divorced man focuses on his personal growth.

It was as though a time bomb was ticking inside of me and I had to get out of the house and out of my marriage and into a completely different type of living situation. I wanted to find another woman who would be compatible with me.

I thought it was going to be nice and easy and I was going to find a girl friend. I thought there was going to be good sex and good love and everything would go just fine. Well, bull. All that didn't happen. It didn't happen at all.

I had imagined myself, most of my life, a fairly unattractive man. I found out at some point, maybe after I was 35, that I was really pretty attractive to women. The message I had been getting from my wife was that I wasn't much. But all of a sudden I was getting attention from other women.

Of course, underneath all this was the theory that a relationship with a woman is *the* important thing in life—and I later found out that's a crock. But the impetus for the first split was to get out of that relationship and get into another relationship with someone who appreciated me, because there was a large community of women, which I had already begun to sample tentatively, that appreciated me.

It didn't work out because the women I was attracted to tended to be a lot more together in the head and emotionally than I was. I was a pretty needing guy at that time. I had a fledgling business that really hadn't started going yet. I'd just quit a salaried job and I'd been out on my own for a year. I had savings that would keep my family going for a year and a half. I had very few clients and I was really pretty scared about that. Every month I saw the bank balance going down. And then to top that all

off, a month after I moved out, I broke my leg. That was pretty traumatic.

Right after that I wanted to be taken back home. My wife took me in and put me in the basement, kept me there for two or three days until I was able to walk on crutches and said, "Out!" I went to the apartment that I'd just leased. I was on crutches for the first time in my life. I spent a lot of time crying and sobbing. I was scared to death because I had always had someone to take care of me emotionally. And now that I really needed taking care of, there was nobody there.

My leg healed. My psyche didn't heal as fast as my leg did. I went through different periods of being absolutely petrified at being alone. I'd never been alone before.

I lived with roommates when I was an undergraduate and got married right after I graduated. The marriage gave me a substitute mother, a person to live with and do the cooking and take care of things. I was always with people. Now here I was for the first time living alone. I had no roommates. I had no wife. I had no mother. I had a broken leg and a business that might or might not be going anywhere.

I was feeling very lonely. I was chasing a lot of women but nothing really satisfactory came up. I didn't have any relationships that I wanted to stick with. I disqualified women one after another after another. I'd get them in bed and then that was pretty much all I wanted from them. And I wouldn't know that until I actually bedded them. Then I realized, This isn't what I want.

I really wanted to go back and live with my family. I wanted to be with my kids. I needed to be with my wife. I had gone through a lot of changes in the year that we lived separately and I figured at that point that I could handle

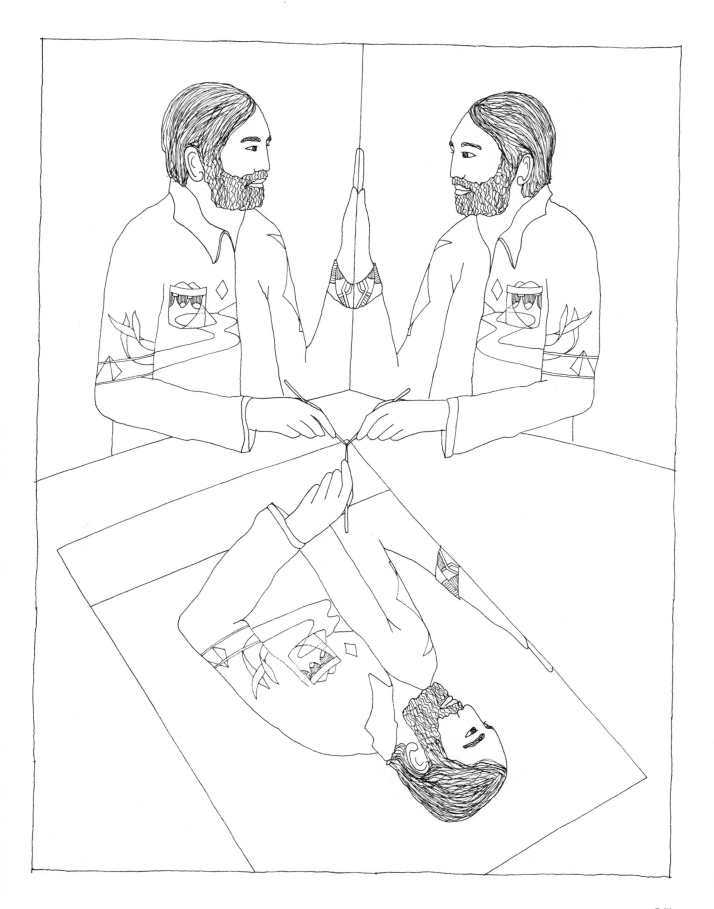

It was as though a time bomb was ticking
inside of me and I had to get out of the house
and out of my marriage.

our relationship. So we got back together.

It wasn't a particularly gratifying relationship but we did a good job with the kids. I didn't want to terminate the marriage. I was in favor of maintaining a very minimal amount of interpersonal contact while still living under the same roof. But after four more years my wife decided, no, she didn't want me around. She needed me out so that she could complete a cycle of *her own* growth. She said she couldn't do it with me there. And that brought about the separation that led to the divorce several years ago.

The impact of not being wanted was difficult to handle, but the separation itself turned out to be pretty easy for me. I went to live with a good friend. We were working in the same office building and he was the guy I was closest to at that time. So that was easy. Also, this time I had no particular expectations. I was saddened that the marriage was going to split up. I felt, "I'm going to be without a family." But that was a kind of "poor me" feeling that went away gradually as I lived alone and did what I did—what I had to do.

Six months after the split I left the city and moved to the country where I own a vineyard. I moved my office up there too. I get my hands dirty, live in Levi's, work the hours I want to, which I love.

Occasionally my ex-wife comes up and drops the kids off for a weekend. I had the oldest boy, who's 21, living with me for about three months, and that was delightful. I wanted him to see if he would like my work, the vineyard work. It's something I could hand down to him. It was a kind of experiment. But he's not ready for that yet. He really

needs to be in the city and on his own. He's got a job now and his own apartment and that's much better than living with the old man and still being a child, because the interaction was that of father and son rather than of peers and friends.

Mostly I'm by myself. I enjoy things like cooking and eating a meal by myself. I'm a creative cook and that's a good pastime. I abhor quickie meals. I always start with fresh food. I eat a lot of vegetables. Sometimes I get famished for meat and I'll go on a meat binge, but generally I'll mix together two or three different fresh vegetables and that's the meal. That and a few glasses of wine.

I may make a nice place setting as though I were having company. If I decide to treat myself and open a bottle of wine that I've had for ten years, then I'll get nice crystal and a nice plate and treat myself to a first-rate meal.

Sometimes I'll read while eating, but the more effort I put into the meal the more likely I am just to concentrate on the food and have that be the primary experience. I don't let other things come in. I just experience the experience of eating.

It's easier to be alone now. But I still haven't come through the woods on being alone. I still get anxious, sometimes, when I'm alone. I'm a great ostrich about it. I avoid looking at what it is that I'm anxious about. I'm really struggling with that one right now. I'd like to lick it. I'd like to be more comfortable with living alone before I start living with somebody else. I use another person to hide from what it is that makes me anxious now, to hide from myself, to hide from what I need to do. I put the energy into relating that I need to put into myself to

I went through different periods
of being absolutely petrified at being alone.

straighten myself out.

So I've said to myself pretty definitely, "No heavy relationship for at least two years." I figure I'm not ready for it. I want to get myself back together again. Really become whole again after this major surgery has been done upon my psyche.

Since the split-up of the marriage I haven't been celibate. I enjoy the company of women and I've had a number of women as friends. I've found that in relationships that tend to get close and intimate I begin to lean emotionally on the person. And I don't like it. I consider that an emotional imbalance. My being emotionally immature is what caused the wreck of my first marriage and I don't want to repeat that.

If it looks as though there's going to be any emotional involvement, if it is more than a casual relationship, then I pretty well state where I am, that I'm not available. And some women are quite resentful of it, especially if they're attracted to me. They want me to be available and dive right into the relationship. I'm not ready for that. I'm not looking for some woman to save me. I've lived with "mother" before. I saw a lot of my mother in my wife.

Still, I don't want to grow old alone. I have visions—yes, just that—I have visions of myself in the future, sitting in front of the fire drinking vintage port and listening to music and chatting with the woman I'm living with.

I'm coming to the conclusion that I'm pretty dissatisfied with myself, with how I'm using my time, with how I'm using my talents. I want to create something or build something. It's not the vineyard that I bought. I thought for a while that it was going to be satisfactory to establish a vineyard, growing fine grapes. But I find that's a pretty shallow goal, and, although it's something that I'm doing and I'm going to do, I'm looking for some other goal. I know I'm not happy with what I'm doing with my time on this earth. What I'm going to do with myself is a kind of greater identity question than just being a father and a businessman and a fine-wine hobbyist. I may be whipping myself. I don't know.

I'm wondering if maybe an attitude shift is what's going to solve the anxiety. Maybe it won't be doing something new but having a little different attitude toward my life. I haven't got the answer. I'm in the middle of this right now. It's existential. It's my existence. Nobody, no psychotherapist, no friend is going to tell me how to solve this one.

I could go back to where I was. I could get a high-paying job. I could get into another relationship. I could occupy myself with those kinds of concerns. But I've been there and I think I know how to handle them. I'm dealing with other concerns that are in my life now and I don't want to run away from them. To me it's a matter of growth.

I could occupy my time bouncing myself off other people and not really having to focus on who I am. I know how to do that. I can get good feedback from people. But that's a narcotic. That's not solving anything. The fact is I'm a goddamn anxious person alone when there aren't people telling me I'm O.K. Until I've learned to solve the problem of living really alone, I think I don't want to come back to those strokes. They'll just seduce me away from learning to live with myself. I choose to deal with that problem. I choose to learn to live with myself.

Pamela's Story

A 32-year-old woman celebrates her self.

I didn't want to be a housewife. My mother was a terrible housewife. My strongest consciousness of her is as a working woman, not a housewife. I think the reason my mother got divorced was that she'd learned all her life to give herself to another human being, a husband, and relied totally upon him, and then she learned finally that the only one you can really rely on is yourself.

My mother and father got divorced when I was 13. Divorce had no meaning for me. I didn't know until after my mother left what it was. Suddenly I didn't have a mother any more. That was very heavy when it happened.

I ended up getting sympathy from friends, and I basked in it. Having a mother leave was more unusual than having a father go. I began to cook for my father; I was playing out this whole dramatic tragic thing and everybody was saying, "Oh, the poor child." I ate it up. Whereas my older sister was really hurting deeply and everybody said that she could take care of herself. Everybody thought I was going to be the one that was the more scarred by it, but I think she was.

I remember one of my very best friends went off to college and, at the end of her first year, she got married. And I thought that was the dumbest thing in the world. I couldn't understand why. I thought he was a jerk. And I remember on her wedding day—I was her maid of honor—she said, "Oh my god, what if I'm not happy?" And I thought, "Honey, there's no way you *can* be happy." Because, again, it was putting it all on somebody else. Aside from the fact that he was a jerk, I don't think you can do that to anybody. And that's what I kept seeing. Somebody saying, "Here, I want you to have my life. We will become one and you will take care of me." And I just didn't see that there was any winning in that situation.

Right now I'm living with a man, but it's so much different from being married. I don't think about words like "expectation" or "commitment." It's more "This is nice. This is pleasant. This is working out in my life." But if it doesn't, if it stops working out, then we'll make other arrangements.

The man I'm involved with right now is in the same theater company I'm in. The relationship started because we were friends. And then we became lovers. There was never a word about a "commitment" to each other. There was a commitment to the company. We lived together part-time for three years. He had a place in the city and I lived at the beach. He came out to teach classes. Then I lost the house I was in, and he got some money, and I found a house that was too expensive for me. It seemed like that was the time to move in together.

I feel very independent in this relationship —more independent than I have in any other. That's because I'm older. It's because of the job I have and autonomy I have. And because of working in the theater and what I've learned from that. In order to go on stage in front of an audience you need to learn to get your own head and body together. And so that's been teaching me a lot.

I get along fairly well with men and I enjoy being around people when I get into that situation. I know that if I weren't with John there would be other men. There are other men around that I'm interested in and yet I don't go into those relationships. I've thought about it.

Sometimes I think about meeting other men. And I just say to myself, It doesn't fit into my life right now. And I like the things that are important in my life. My needs are satisfied right now.

When I'm not with a man I tend to spend more time with women, which I like a lot. But I also find it very frustrating because I've found that with women it's always been a case of, "Sure, I'd love to. I don't have anything better to do." As much as we talk about Women's Lib, I still hear that. I've gotten hurt in relationships with women. I have had friendships with women that have been as rewarding as with any man. And I've gotten hurt because I'll have this relationship and as soon as a man comes into the scene, I, as a woman, become second. I'm told, "See you around, George is here. You wouldn't expect me to give up George, would you?"

It's just as true with hip women as with any other. Maybe women who are really heavy

into Women's Lib don't do it, but they are too heavy for me. I mean, I really don't want to sit around all night and talk about how awful men are.

My life goes in phases whether I'm living with somebody or not. It changes. I go through periods, maybe two or three weeks, maybe a month, in which I'm totally social and want to be with people constantly. I'll feel a great need for people, for warmth and affection and all the rest of it. There's a certain amount of madness in it which I like. I go out and I'm very open and very affectionate and I make a lot of friends. At the end of that I feel very satisfied and I go back to being alone and working.

People I've been very open with will come around then and say, "Well, here I am again," and I'll just say, "No, you don't understand, I'm working now. That was just a phase. I mean, it was very nice but it doesn't mean anything long term . . . ." This is partly the

Saying you're lonely is saying you're not communicating; you're not talking to anybody including yourself.

reason I wouldn't want to be married. I change too much. I change too much day to day.

I've lived alone for periods as long as a year and a half. The time I've been with John we've lived apart as much or more than we've lived together. I've learned to treat myself well alone.

Once a friend of mine told me about a night when she was alone, and she cooked all the things she really loved, and she got herself a nice bottle of wine and just treated herself. After I talked to her, one night I cooked a roast chicken with potatoes just for me. I got a really good bottle of wine, put on music, ate dinner, and then afterwards I danced for three hours. It was one of the most totally perfect evenings I'd ever spent. It was like taking myself on a date. I began to realize that one of the absolute beauties of being alone, of living alone, is that you can do anything you want, anytime, for as long as you want.

Our culture says, starting from masturbation onward: "Do not love thyself. Love other people. Giving is better than receiving." And there's always this feeling of doing for others. It just doesn't occur to you that you can do things for yourself. In the beginning I found it hard to take from myself. And it was hard to give to myself. But it was a really nice feeling at the end of that evening to say, "What a nice evening. Thank you. That was perfect."

Dancing by myself in public is another thing I've learned to do. I really love to dance. There was a big dance a couple of weeks ago. It wasn't any big deal but I really wanted to dance and I went down there and I danced, all by myself. Fortunately, there's a lot of craziness in this town, and it allows me to do something and no-

body's going to lock me up. If I did that in a bar somewhere else, people would think I was loony, dancing by myself for three hours.

I came home at the end of the dance totally exhilarated. I couldn't have had a better time. John was at home and he was watching television. It wouldn't have been right trying to lay a trip on him to go to a dance that he didn't want to do and wouldn't enjoy. And it wouldn't have been right for me to stay home and watch television, which I wouldn't enjoy. We really do keep that straight. And sometimes we have to remind each other that it's getting confused again, and say, "Wait a minute. We're starting to compromise." Compromise. That's a big word that couples love to use. Compromise means "O.K. We won't do what you want to do and we won't do what I want to do. We'll both be unhappy." That's compromise. And it's dumb.

On my 30th birthday I went down to the beach alone. I was sort of prepared for something awful to happen. A roommate of mine went crazy when she turned 30. I took a walk on the beach and it was absolutely spectacular. It was just beautiful. Everything was perfect. The sun was setting. The moon was coming up. The birds were doing this number in the sky. There was not another soul on the beach, and I thought, "There's nobody else seeing this. And that's perfectly all right, because I'm big enough, I'm important enough that all this can be happening and I appreciate it. I appreciate it enough as one person to make it all worth it. However big the ocean is and the world is, I'm big enough to appreciate it." That day, on the beach, I got a sense of eternity. It was a flash so powerful that I realized loneli-

However big the ocean is and the world is, I'm big enough to appreciate it.

ness was only a phase. I guess it has to do with dying.

I think "I feel lonely" is really saying, "I feel out of touch. I'm not relating to anything." And I think that that can mean not relating to yourself, too.

I do feel lonely sometimes, but it never gets overpowering. I'll take a walk on a beach, which I do a lot, and when I come back I don't feel lonely any more, because a communication has happened. It doesn't *always* happen but a lot of times it does. Most people think that going to a bar is a cure for loneliness. Occasionally it can work out. The right circumstances can happen. But you're really putting it in somebody else's hands because you're going there with nothing to offer and expecting something to happen. You're really asking for a miracle. But the source is in you; you've just got to get back in touch with it.

Sex is right up there with eating, drinking, and walking on the beach. I don't give it any more weight, but it certainly is as important. I guess some of the needs that I felt when I was younger were satisfied by sex. Now I still have the same number of needs but they're satisfied by different things, like walking on the beach, or the work I do in the theater, the dancing, the warm-up exercises. They are very sensual experiences so I get a lot of satisfaction from those things.

I'm no good at one-night stands. I haven't had much success at them. All I want to do is get laid and then I want the man to disappear in the morning. Unfortunately he doesn't. He's there. And I have to deal with some guy who says, "When can I see you again?" And I want to say, "You can't, honey. This was it.

Didn't you understand? Didn't I make it perfectly clear?" I haven't done it very often. I feel silly afterwards more than anything.

I have the best sex with people that I've known beforehand. A sense of humor is really important to me. And it's important to me in sex too. Everybody's got to realize, especially the first time, it's going to be awkward and silly and you better be able to laugh about it and say, "This is kind of weird. Where do we go from here?" It's like dancing with somebody for the first time: "How do you move? Which dance do you do?"

My dog gives me an immense amount of satisfaction and companionship. Sometimes I just want to spend a weekend alone—I mean alone, not with anybody. The dog's outside and I'm in the house doing whatever. And then we'll take a walk. And it really is that feeling that there are just two of us in this world—Moose and me—and we're both sharing the same thing right now. Maybe in a different way.

I talk about him in the same way that people talk about their kids. In fact, somebody will say, "Oh, my kid did such and such," and I'll go, "You know, Moose does the same thing." And suddenly I'm thinking, Oh, Lord, I'm getting into one of those weird things. They're going to think I have him running around in little booties and stuff. I mostly treat him like a dog. I don't get things confused.

I have no desire to have children. I think I discovered the major reason why I would never need to have children. It's partly because of the theater thing. We did a play called "Delicate Balance" by Edward Albee and I played Claire who is a 50-year-old alcoholic. It

It was like taking myself
out on a date.

was a very hard part. She is a very rich character, and because I liked the play and I liked her I really wanted her to be something important. And she was. It was every bit as important as giving birth. I created her from nothing—with the help of Edward Albee. I brought her to life. And I think that's the creative process. There are many ways you can have that feeling. I'm not saying one is more important than another. I do believe you need it. I do believe that your life will not be as full if you don't have it. Somehow there's got to be that feeling of bringing forth something that, before you brought it forth, did not exist.

I have to say at this point I would never get married, certainly not by the state and certainly not by religion. I'm not religious and I don't believe in the state telling me whether I am or am not married. So it would never be any kind of legal or religious bond.

I have a hard time imagining being with somebody for the rest of my life. It's not something that is a horrible thought to me, as long as I could keep growing and moving and as long as the two of us didn't stop each other.

I think there'll be some person or other. I believe that if I want to be with somebody I'll be able to. And if I don't, that'll be O.K. That'll be because I want to be alone.

Most women do grow old alone. Married women inevitably outlive their husbands. If anything, it's harder on them than it would be on someone who's always been single. I don't think I'll have a hard time. It doesn't scare me. If something happened to John I would be very, very sad. It would be just terrible. But I could live without him. I wouldn't fall apart.

Right now I'm happy to be living with somebody rather than spending too much time alone. We have a lot of freedom. He's got his own bedroom and an office space that's his. And I've got my room upstairs.

We program in time to be alone. Sometimes we eat together and sometimes we don't. If I'm down there fixing dinner and he comes in I'll invite him, and vice versa. He hasn't slept in his bedroom much, I have to admit. That's only because we're getting along really well right now. But it's nice to know he has a room to go to.

I think you tend to have fewer fights if you realize that you need space. I really believe that people have fights on purpose for no other reason than to get away. I know that I was doing that. I was creating fights just because I wanted to be alone, and I didn't know how to get out of the house. So I'd have a fight, that was easy, and then run out. Now it's perfectly all right for me to say or for him to say, "I want to be alone tonight. You sleep downstairs. I just feel like being alone."

I guess more than ever I want to figure out ways of being able to find the sources inside myself. That doesn't mean I'll never need people any more. I think it's bad to get into a place where you don't need people. I can see myself getting into that place, and I don't think I want to. I want to keep that option open.

I go through phases when I'm really strong. There are a lot of people who come to me then. But when you do feel strong it's really nice to be able to bring a few other people up with you, because when you go down again there's that good feeling of being able to grab hold of somebody else.

Cindy's Story

A 24-year-old woman searches for loving relationships.

I think about growing old alone. When I was a little kid my mother told me she didn't get married until she was 29. I thought "Oh, that's old. I don't want to be that old before I get married." I'm going to be 25 pretty soon and I start seeing myself as getting old. Part of me is saying, "Cool it. Loosen up. The liberated way to think about this is to realize it doesn't matter how old you are when you get married."

But there's this other little voice that tells me, "You're getting on, Cindy." I feel some pressure now that I'm reaching the quarter-century mark and I'm not in love with anybody. It reminds me of a horoscope I once read that told me, "You'll die alone." I said, "Oh, no. I want to be with somebody."

I have often lived by myself and I enjoy that. I like not having anybody see what I do. If I'm going to do something completely lazy, I like it that nobody knows what I'm doing. Nobody can say, "What's wrong with you? You're so unintellectual, lying there in the bathtub watching the tube." If I'm going to do something really awful, like eat three chocolate-chip cookies in a row, nobody is going to know.

Another nice thing is not having to go home at a certain time for dinner. I've lived with people in a house where you were sort of expected to come home and share dinner. I prefer being completely on my own so on the spur of the moment I can go out and do whatever I want. I like not having to tell people where I'm going. I like having time to think. When I've lived in a house with a bunch of people, I've often felt responsible for carrying on a conversation with them when I would rather be by myself with just my own thoughts.

And then there's the need for privacy. For instance, I go crazy if I can't masturbate. When my mother visited me for a week last year, the only time I could masturbate was when she was in the shower. That was not enough. I have to have about three orgasms a day or I just can't stand it. So when I have no privacy, it bugs me.

I don't like to compare masturbating to having sex with another person. It is a completely different thing. It doesn't take the place of being with a man.

Unfortunately, it is very difficult meeting men. I spend eight hours a day working in a very small company. There's no one new there to meet. And I never meet anybody new through my friends because I know my friends. I know the friends of my friends. I've gone out with all of them that I can go out with.

Then there are courses at the college. But I don't want to take a course just to meet a man. I want to take courses that I'm interested in. The problem is that the courses I'm interested in do not draw men.

So I go to bars. It is very easy to meet men in bars. I could write a whole book about bars. My friends say, "How can you go to a bar? You'll never meet anybody in a bar." The people who say this are the same ones who can't go to a movie or out to eat by themselves. But I can. And I generally can tell which men are going to last one night and which are going to call me again.

I go through phases of wanting to be married and phases of wanting to stay single. When I was in high school I planned to find someone in college and get married right away. I thought all the boys in my town were creeps. But when I got to college I found just as many

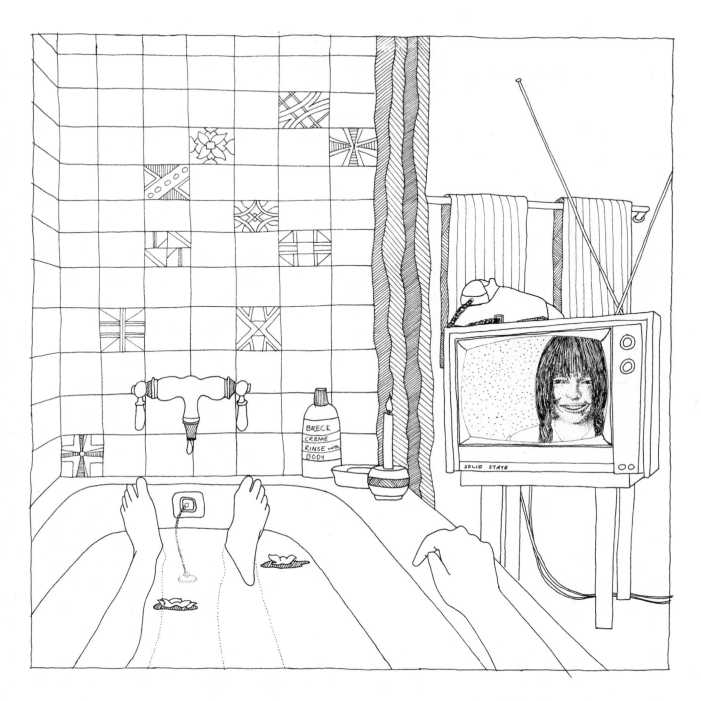

guys I thought were creeps.

After about two years in college I decided "This is it. I am never going to get married." And I just took it for granted from then on that I was going to be single for the rest of my life. And I was really happy thinking about that, thinking about being single. I thought that that was the way of life for me. I was going to concentrate on finding a career. Just concentrate on myself. Then, shortly after that, I met

a guy and I thought I might marry him. And I would have married him if he had asked, which he didn't. Which was lucky as I look back on it.

And that is the pattern in my life. When I meet a man that I'm interested in, I forget about my dreams. But when there is no man in my life, I am very happy being single. I dream a lot more and I believe in my dreams. I believe I can do them.

Karl's Story

A 68-year-old divorced man deals with aging.

The first six years of my life I spent without any peers. I think I developed a tendency to be by myself which has lasted, I guess, down to the present. It's rather difficult to make contact with people. That's the pattern.

I didn't plan to be single when I entered my 60s. I would have much preferred to have continued living with my second wife if it had been possible. But it was too unequal a relationship. I couldn't have possibly continued under those circumstances with her. It was just too damned painful. I would have probably ended up an alcoholic. I felt like I was being pushed out; it was such a cold relationship. The marriage had ended quite a few years earlier. We were just living together, going through the motions.

So I decided that when the first opportunity came, I would leave. Just one month before our 20th anniversary I was offered a new job and I took it. I was 60. I would have left much earlier but I hadn't been earning enough money to be able to pay her alimony and still get along myself.

For me it was a difficult time, being alone again. I guess it wasn't very hard on her. But I have a tendency to be overly dependent because I was very dependent on my mother and that was the pattern that developed over my lifetime. So for a couple of years it was just really hellish, particularly since I had moved to a different city and I didn't know anybody. I'd just go to the office and go back to my little apartment and have to spend the time by myself.

Eventually, I made some friends in the office. Then I made some friends away from the office, too, and got a small circle of friends going. Even so, the transition was so difficult that I got into a period of depression.

I realized that I had to fight this thing through by myself and use all the resources at my command. My resources were not so much social at that time but artistic. I used my creativity to help me cope with those periods of loneliness and depression.

The main thing I learned then was I had to be more self-reliant. This was very, very difficult for me to do. I had a tendency to rely on a love relationship. I began to see that I had to have my own resources right inside of myself in order to cope, that you really couldn't depend on anybody, that you had to learn to make your way through life primarily with your own resources.

It was an emotional reorientation more than anything else. In fact, I was somewhat infantile. I was in a state the Freudians call "infantile regression." I was still at the stage where when a loved person left me I would feel like I did when my mother left me when I was ten years old. I just felt devastated and terribly alone in the universe. It's been a long process to get to the point where now I'm able to realize that I'm not entirely alone in the universe—that there are people out there for me—and be able to manage my own life fairly well.

In day-to-day details I was probably less prepared for taking care of myself than any male ever was. I didn't know a goddamn thing about housekeeping. I didn't know how to cook. I didn't know what to do with the house. I didn't know anything about laundry. I had to improvise as I went along. That was quite an interesting period.

I think that almost every man should have to do all these things for himself for at least a

year so that he realizes the contribution that his wife makes—that is, if she is staying home and doing these things. I tried to share with my ex-wife but she wouldn't allow me. She was very impatient. She wouldn't take the time to teach me.

I started doing all these things for myself right from the beginning. I just went ahead and tried it, that's all. I'm sure that other people would have done a better job. I was content. I didn't expect gourmet meals. I cleaned the house whenever it got so damned dirty that I couldn't stand it any more. Once in a while I got a little help from friends. Friends' children would come over and help me when it needed a thorough cleaning.

I never did get to do a real neat job of mending my own pants or holes in my shirts and stuff like that. They still look a little bit amateurish when I get through with my mending. But I'm glad I learned to sew. It helps to pass the time. And I kind of like to use my hands. Hand-and-mind coordinating is a satisfaction to me.

A few years after my divorce I was forced to retire. I didn't like my life at all. So I decided I wanted one big last final adventure. And the thing that appealed to me the most was just to take a chance and uproot myself completely and start all over again.

So I packed up and moved back to my homeland, to Austria. As it turned out, for medical and Social Security reasons, I couldn't stay there after all. But it had been my intention to live out my retirement there. I think that the problems of aging are dealt with with a good deal more humanity and compassion in Europe than they are in the United States. There's a great awareness, and the governments are willing to set the money aside for those needs.

There is an atmosphere of more awareness of an older person's shortcomings. And perhaps there is more of a sense of interdependence. We are taught in the United States that we are rugged individuals and we shouldn't depend on anybody else, turn to anybody else for help. And we're even taught that we, as

In day-to-day details I was probably less prepared for taking care of myself than any male ever was.

older people, shouldn't become dependent on our children at all for any kind of help or support. You don't have this excess individualism in the old country. I think they accept the fact that older people do need a little bit of help.

In Vienna practically every neighborhood has an older person's club—neighborhood places where you can come and drink a beer or a glass of wine in the evening and meet and talk with other people even if you don't have any relatives. There's a chance for socializing in those taverns. Of course, the other thing is that you can go out at night and feel perfectly safe anywhere you are. So those are other ways that I think life is made a little bit more comfortable for the older person.

I was really touched a couple of times when I was over there by people who were older than I and who would reach out and ask me to help them. I thought this was wonderful, that they were willing to admit that they were weaker and that they needed a little help to cross the street. One day I was sauntering down the street and an older man came up to me and asked me if I could help him down the street, give him my arm for several blocks until he got where he wanted to go. And I thought that was really wonderful.

Well, I'm right in the middle of growing old alone, and I'm learning how to do it gracefully. I think. It's more or less an intuitive thing rather than a conscious effort, although I do spend some time in introspection and see my life in perspective—something I never did when I was young. Then it was just one damned thing after the other without any sense of relationship. Now I've got a continuity.

I had a sort of mystical experience that helped me with that when I was in Austria. I always get emotional about going back to my childhood surroundings. It's so beautiful and so poignant. I suppose since I really had no father or mother to speak of that I turned to my homeland as my father and mother. It's like I'm going back to father and mother every time I go back there. There are so many beautiful things over there that I enjoy and that are a source of daily delight.

There's one particular region, very lovely, right near Vienna. It's just one enchanting village after the other, all along the Danube. There are little hills there, and many castles; every little town and village is entrancing. And I decided to go back to retrace a trip that I had taken 40 years ago.

The town most sharply etched in my memory was a little one that's famous as having been the place where Richard the Lionhearted was held as a captive. I climbed up all those ruins that I had climbed up before by myself 40 years ago. I could get a wonderful view, in both directions, of the Danube below me, and the lovely little village with its spire from the church and all the little homes and shops and their fascinating rooftops.

And, as I looked down, the stream suddenly turned into my own life. It just seemed like I relived my entire life from childhood to the present as that river flowed past. For the first time I realized that everything had happened the way it had to happen and that everything was interrelated in my life. And that I had no reason whatsoever to blame myself or feel guilty about past misdeeds or things that I had done to other people. It just couldn't have come in any other way. And there was this

I used my creativity to help me cope with those periods of loneliness and depression.

wonderful sense of awareness of the interconnectedness of all human experience, particularly in my own life, which has stayed with me. It was like a great burden of guilt for sins I had committed against people was lifted from me when I saw that all this might have been planned eons and eons ago. There was the sense of connectedness. It was quite a mystical experience. It seemed like my whole life transpired in what may have been just a very few minutes. I have no idea, really, how long it took. It might have taken half an hour. It might have taken half a minute. And that was the one time when I can truly say that I had *Satori*, what the Buddhists call *Satori*, which is a sudden intuition of Truth.

Since I came back to the United States I've gotten active in a number of volunteer activities which have brought friends into my life. One of them was that I took on the design job for a group of poets that publishes a magazine. Then, through my work with the United Farm Workers, I got to know other people. And through friends I get to meet other friends. Friends mean a great deal to me because I don't have any living relatives, except a cousin in Budapest. If I didn't have some friends I don't know that I could stand it.

I don't join groups just to find friends. I am primarily interested in doing the work. I happen to have liked poetry ever since I was introduced to it by a young friend of mine when I was a young man, so it just occurred to me when I heard that this group was going to get out a publication to offer my services as a typographic designer.

I'm also involved in something called co-counseling. It's a self-help community that was founded way back about a quarter of a century ago for mutual support. It's all over the world actually, but concentrated on the West Coast. It started in Seattle, Washington, and grew to embrace Oregon and also California. We've got about 300 members around here.

You're encouraged to talk about any distress or any good things for an hour. Each one talks about the thing that's closest to him. And you're encouraged to what they call "discharge." There are four primary kinds of "discharges": yawning, laughing, anger—real indignant anger—and shedding tears. This helps us to get rid of big loads of emotional blockages and past griefs and we get over our distresses in this way. And we're given a good deal of love and attention from our co-counselor. Most people do this counseling once a week or more. I do it, although my distresses of course are far less than they were before.

Most of my friends are, I guess, in couples. In fact, most of my friends are in families and I enjoy the company of their children as well. I've been sort of adopted as a surrogate grandpa by at least one family and maybe a second.

I'm living in an apartment complex for retired people. It has some advantages. In case of an accident I can call on someone. The rent is subsidized, which is a very important factor because I have a small income. But I don't like the segregation. I'd prefer an arrangement whereby I had contact more often with people in other age groups. If I had my choice, I would like to live with a family if it were possible to find some family that would like to have me

It's been a long process to get to the point where now I realize that I'm not entirely alone in the universe.

around. I think it's pretty difficult to find this type of a situation. It's a very difficult meshing of likes and dislikes and life styles.

I've got one little thing going now that I enjoy a great deal. One of my friends comes over once a week and she brings her daughter. And I either spend time with her or with the daughter doing some kind of craft activity. I may teach her calligraphy or work on a stamp collection with her. I'm quite a stamp collector and I've got a lot of extra stamps and I'm helping show her how to put the stamps in place. I have some drawing materials there for her too.

My friends primarily are younger than I am. I have only a very few friends that are in my own age bracket. I feel more at home with younger people because too many older people are pretty conservative and my views are more in line with those of the younger generation. In other words I believe in change and I believe things should be done to improve the American way of life, which I think in many ways is a pretty damn inhumane way of life. I find more younger people than older people who are aware of this and want to do something about changing the situation.

Also, when it comes to things that I enjoy, music or the arts, I'm a little more progressive. Most older people tend to be more conservative in those areas also. I've got more in common with the viewpoint of the younger generation generally speaking.

I do get lonely. There are a number of evenings I have to spend all by myself. And there are some that are especially difficult. I do make telephone calls now and then when I'm alone. It's fun to talk to people over the telephone. That helps me to

forget a little bit, forget myself. Now and then the radio is a help. And I have quite a record collection that I can call on. Then, of course, there's going back into earlier experiences in your life. I'll haul out some of the more pleasant ones for reliving. But sometimes you've just got to suffer through it; there's no other way than to suffer. You just have to endure.

I'll talk to myself, get a kind of interior monologue going. The kinds of things that I talk to myself about very often are things that I don't get to talk about with anybody else. Like many of the experiences that I've had overseas, particularly as a child. Another thing that I do is observe myself as a child as though I were on the outside watching myself. I see myself going around the streets with my hand in grandma's hand looking around in various episodes of my early childhood.

I try to manage to avoid being alone at Christmas time. I plan to be with friends. About my birthday, I don't really care too much. I don't pay any attention to it.

There have been many times and occasions when I've really enjoyed being alone. I remember one time when I went through this little village in Austria, not far from Vienna. And I was just so absolutely entranced by all the details of everything that I saw. Oh, it just seemed like everything was a product of joy; it wasn't simply built to make money. I remember after taking this walk I sat down in the plaza and shouted, "Joy, joy, joy."

Being alone has gotten harder for me over the years. It wasn't at all a problem when I was young. I could spend endless hours by myself. There was no limit. But I feel the pressure of loneliness much more acutely at the present time than I did before. I need human beings more.

Carole's Story

A 38-year-old divorced mother makes her new life work.

My husband went off with a 24-year-old cocktail waitress. I was very surprised when it happened. I always thought that I would be married "until death do us part." It was the first year that the no-fault divorce law went into effect. My husband's father had just died and I think that it made him go into an identity crisis, the male menopause or whatever you want to call it, earlier than his contemporaries.

But now so many of my friends find themselves in the same situation. Five years ago it was a shock to everyone—ours was one of the first divorces among our group. I didn't see any problem in our relationship. I think that we both thought we had a pretty good marriage for nine years. As a matter of fact, I believed I was the only one who could get along with my ex-husband. I felt secure.

The hardest things at first were the hurt and the guilt. I'd wonder if it was my fault. And there was depression. It wasn't the physical logistics of being single that was hard. I fell into that very easily.

I did worry at night at the very beginning about being alone with just the kids. So I signed up with the rental agency of a local university, and since then I've always had students boarding with me.

I was already seeing a therapist at the time of the split about something other than my marriage. So when my husband left I just continued therapy, dealing with all that new depression and guilt. I was in therapy for 18 months. I think it really helped me, because the therapist was so much more objective than other people I talked to. And I talked to everybody, including the milkman and the mailman. My ex-husband would die if he knew how much I talked. But it was cathartic. I had to talk. And I think that's what made my recovery faster.

Another thing I did was to read copiously, just about every self-help book that came along. Most of them were marriage manuals, which was kind of ridiculous. But I read them to find where I'd gone wrong. The books showed me that I really hadn't gone wrong.

I didn't burn my bridges right away because I was always hoping that my husband would tire of his girl friend. It took about two years to overcome that idea.

After he left there was pressure from a lot of sources to go out and find another man, not necessarily another mate. I felt it inwardly—"I'm not a real woman; I've been rejected; I've got to prove to myself that I still am alluring."

I used to say to friends, "When are you going to fix me up?" But now I say, "Don't bother." Because I'm more comfortable. I'm comfortable now without a man on my arm. It used to be embarrassing, because I figured everyone was thinking, "Well, the reason your husband left is because you're frigid, if you're not sleeping with somebody." But Women's Lib has given me confidence, too. Now I don't care what they think.

And as for sex, I haven't had any for two years. And that doesn't bother me. I think sex is habit-forming—that is, when you're out of the habit, you miss it less. I don't know if this is true for men, but I cannot imagine my ex-husband being celibate for two years. Every once in a while I'll think about flirting with the appliance man who's fixing my garbage disposal or something, but never enough to really do anything about it.

I talked to everybody, including the milkman and the mailman. My ex-husband would die if he knew how much I talked.

Still, I feel like I'm a very sexual animal. I know that I'm in my sexual prime. But I also feel that as a person I'm too good to just spread myself around like a bitch in heat. If I have a relationship with a man, then I want a lot of sex. And the same with masturbation. But the less you do, the less you want. I feel that my physical need for sex is kind of wound down.

My children were six and nine when we split up. They immediately became very helpful and mothered me while I was passed out on the couch for three months. My daughter held in her emotions, wouldn't tell her friends. It embarrassed her. She wasn't going to tell anybody, she said. Then one morning, two months after the break, she had hysterics in school. It all came out.

We haven't had any professional counseling as a family but we've always been very open, and I've tried to have the kids express anything they want to me. I've also been open with them. I know most of their feeling and they know what's going on with me. And consequently it's a very intimate relationship we have. There's a sense of total companionship I get from them. I even watch TV with them.

I read a poll where 70 percent of the parents that answered said they would not have children if they could do it again. Now that blew my mind. I think it's a symptom of our society, where it's "me, me, me." Everything for me. I feel that the biggest joy of my life is my children.

I find being a parent easier now than when I was married, because my husband was another child and there was a lot of conflict between my real children and this adult child that I had.

My ex-husband is free to see the kids any time he wants. It ends up being just once a week. In the beginning, when he was living with, and not wed to, his girl friend, he was embarrassed by that. He didn't want his children to know it. And I went along with it too because it would be hard to explain. So all their meetings were at our house, and I left. It was good for the kids because then they had all their toys and they could act normally. To this day they spend a lot of time with him here at home.

I have deliberately chosen not to get a full-time job while the children are still at home. I feel sometimes like time is closing me in and I should get a job because who's going to employ me after I'm 40. But it's more important to be with my children when they need me. And I think that children under 12 really need a parent to be on call. I'm not against mothers working. But I think that would distress my children because they're happy when I'm there watching them at soccer games or school programs. And it's important to them that I'm here when they come home.

The kids love their father very much. But they see his faults and know that life is a lot simpler without him under foot. If you were to ask them if they'd like me to be married to someone else they'd probably say no, because they have a cushy situation. They get my attention. They're free to do what they want. They only have one authority to deal with.

When I have dated, my daughter has hated it. She was very jealous that I was going out. Or maybe she felt annoyed because she thought I was being disloyal to her father. Whereas my son, he's always been in-

terested in the fellow and hasn't seemed to care.

I had a man sleep over a few times, but it's just too scary. It's just not worth it. Particularly now that my daughter's a teenager and knows what's going on, I just wouldn't do it. And also I think that her opinion of me would diminish. When you're an adolescent you think of your parents as being pure and not even having sex. You're very idealistic. When she gets into college it'll be a whole different situation. I'll do anything I want.

If I had sex away from home, it'd be all right. I don't think it's dirty. But if my daughter asked me if I were sleeping with anybody, I'd say "No," even if I were having sex. I don't see why I should complicate her emotions.

Right now I consider my being single permanent. There are some good things about being single. I like my privacy. That's one thing I'm kind of jealous of now, and I'd really have to be madly in love with somebody to give it up. Now I can

Before the divorce my concerns were the wax build-up on the floor and what am I going to cook tonight and is my husband happy?

fart in bed and not worry about it. And, if I were married, I'd have to worry about my teeth, my breath. Maybe people don't any more, but when I was a new bride you worried about things like that.

Being alone has been good for me. I am more well-rounded; I am more self-reliant, more interesting. I now attempt things that I would never do before. My sewing machine used to scare me because I couldn't thread it properly without reading the manual. Now I will fix the TV antenna when it blows down.

I like the feeling of being competent. It's a lot better than having to call up somebody at $27 an hour to come out and fix the sliding door. I'm pleased with myself. I'm proud. And I think it's a good example for both my children to see that I can do things. I went to night school and learned the skills that I needed to start my own business, which I work on, part-time, out of my home.

Before the divorce my concerns were the wax build-up on the floor and what am I going to cook tonight and is my husband happy? I can't remember what I used to think about when I would drive along in the car. I must have thought about something unless I just hummed a merry tune. But it's been blocked out of my memory. Or else my mind was a blank. It probably was.

Now my mind is constantly whirring around, buzzing. I think about everything. It can be about how I'm going to handle a problem around the house. Or, now that my daughter's a teenager, things to do with her growing awareness of being a woman.

I'll probably be lonely on occasion if I never marry again. And I'll be envious of other people once in a while. But when I look around at my friends' husbands, I often feel a sense of relief that I'm not stuck with this or that s.o.b. I'd rather be by myself than be in most situations.

I think about growing old alone all the time. But I'm glad that I'm growing old without my ex-husband because I think he's going to be an ornery old man. And it's going to serve his young bride right when she's stuck with him later on.

I miss the intimacy with a man. It's different from the intimacy with your sister or your mother. The challenge of the intimacy and the rewards and the fun. You can be very close to your children. You can read their thoughts. But you can't go through life continually being intimate with your children.

That intimacy, it's everything. Just that little look that you have—"Ah yes, I know what you mean." And sharing your aspirations. But then, on the other hand, when I read or watch a movie or a TV show that I'm really moved by, I might be embarrassed if another person, another adult, were in that same room with me, even if it were my husband. Because I cannot cry in front of people. By myself, as a single person, I can let myself go and really get emotional over something that I read or see on TV. But when I cry and there's somebody in the room, I kind of feel like covering up.

I even feel embarrassed crying in front of my kids. When I read them *Charlotte's Web* and the spider died at the end, I was crying. And they were flanking me, looking at me in a kind of odd, questioning way—"How can you cry over a spider?" Do you think that if I were with somebody that did cry in such circumstances and he was crying and I was crying, that we'd be able to cry freely after a few years?

Claudia's Story

A 60-year-old woman remarries her former husband but continues to live alone.

I was at a fair outside the community center and I was wandering around. A man, standing there, said, "Are you alone? I mean, do you have somebody, a man in your life?" Apparently it was some kind of invitation. A nice little man about my age, in his 60s.

And I said, "I have a very good friend, yes. In fact, I'm married but I live by myself. I'm not closed to the outside world."

A woman who was nearby said, "That sounds interesting. I'd like to hear more about that. Can I come talk to you one day?"

Frank and I were married for ten years. We got divorced five years ago and we didn't have much to do with one another for a period of time. Eventually, he found someone else and moved to another city.

I remember the day he told me he was going. I was really devastated. I knew we always would be attracted to one another. I couldn't put any demands on him but I told him before he left that I would like to be his mistress sometime if he felt like having something like that going. I was very sad. I felt, Now I'm really losing him completely.

But half a year later he let me know that it hadn't worked out with his new friend. By that time I had bought my own house. He called me and asked if he could move in with me for a little while until he found a place for himself, which he soon did. And since then our relationship has been pretty much like it is today.

He lives in an apartment nearby. We meet a couple times a week, two or three times as it happens. We will usually try to make our appointments with other people accordingly. He goes out with some other ladies that he dates and I go out with some other men. But he's my priority and I'm his priority. We do enjoy several things very much together. We enjoy going to the beach. We enjoy listening to music.

Sometimes he will come and suggest that he repair a door for me. But if I ask him, "Why don't you also cut my lawn?" he'll say, "Oh, no." I think he's afraid that I'll be spoiled if he starts doing too many things for me.

He may call and say, "You want to come over for dinner? I made a nice meat sauce." He's developed into an excellent cook, this man who would never boil an egg. He didn't want to put his foot in the kitchen.

We spend the night together maybe once a week. I would like it if we did it more than we do, because I like to sleep next to him. He has gotten certain habits by living alone.

About three or four months ago he proposed to me. He said, "I'm not going to get down on my knees but . . . ." He asked me to be remarried so that I would be eligible to receive his Social Security, which he has worked for during his whole life. He did it because he loves me. And I felt, Yes, why not? I don't intend to remarry in general. I'm perfectly pleased the way I live my life now, as long as everything can stay as it was. So, he even renewed the lease on his apartment for another year, and we got married. He lives in his place and I live in mine.

When we were married before I wasn't ready for a relationship like this. I was too jealous. It's something I've done quite a lot of work with. It has always been easier for him to say, "Listen, if you want to do something

I couldn't really find myself
when I was married.

outside our marriage, just don't tell me. But I don't mind it at all." I would have minded it then. But I don't mind whatever he does now, because it's not part of me. I realize I can't be with him all the time. There are other things in other people that I can't substitute for. And he can't substitute for some other things that I might want to have in my life. I'm not talking about sexual things. I have three other very good men friends, like buddies, and none of them really has any great importance to me sexually.

Living apart helped me get over my jealous feelings. It wasn't that I was deeply jealous, but I just felt that it was some kind of cheating when he'd be with other women. I was quite severe about that, earlier. I don't really know how it changed. In part it happened because I worked with myself. I think I got over it also by realizing that I am the central woman in his life, and by realizing that I sometimes need to see other people too, more than I used to. My life is different. I seem to just let things happen more. I could never be happy now with a conventional marriage. I think I have a very rich life. If we were living together I would be more jealous. I can't quite see how you could do the kind of thing we're doing, living this way, when you live in the same house together, when you hear the door, when you know when the person leaves and you lie awake and listen for him to come back. There must be something very difficult in doing it when you're living together. I know a couple that

does it, has an open marriage while living in the same house together. I can't quite see how I could be a part of a setup like that.

When I was married before I always felt, Why the hell do I always have to do all the work? Why do I have to make the marriage go? Why do I do all the placating, trying to do things differently so I won't irritate the other person, trying to be more forgiving, all kinds of ways of trying, all that work? I think women have a much stronger desire to work with themselves than men do. But sometimes working on a marriage, if you're the only one doing it, can work against your own growth. I couldn't really find myself when I was married. I have found myself after being on my own.

You know, I think there's something very truthful to the idea that, until you know for sure that you can live by yourself, you aren't really quite fit enough to live with somebody else. Until you've explored whatever there might be inside you, deep things you've never really encountered before, until you've done that, maybe you shouldn't live with another person.

My feeling is that as we get older it might happen that we'll live together again. It would have to be in a large place, because we're used to our own space. And it's awfully nice to be able to say, "Listen you're not in a very good mood today. And I can't do much for you. You're sort of pushing me away. So I'm just going to be on my own."

Mark's Story

A 28-year-old artist immerses himself in his work.

Thoreau is the model for my life. He lived at that pond and really was in touch with all the waves that his own life created. Every ripple of his life was taken care of, and he got to know it all. *Walden* is an inspiration to me for the style of life that I want to live now. Thoreau put straight ideas about loneliness. His book and his life at the pond have really inspired me in a lot of ways to live the way I want to live. Right now I have certain things that I want to achieve and they're pretty ambitious things. I really am putting a lot of energy into my work. It's fairly exhausting.

I'm an architect. I went to school in Europe where I was really successful. The taste of that success is something fairly difficult to deal with because it makes you want more and more. There, I was like a big fish in a small sea. I've found being in the United States very different. In the States I've found many people who are very good at what I do. There's much more competition. So I'm in a very tough situation.

After 18 months here I'm really starting to feel that I'm getting closer to where I want to be and things are starting to happen. I won't rest until I do what I want to do. So basically my life centers around that—my work. Even my relationships involve people who are involved in architecture.

I work at home. I like working and living in the same place. I wash my pens in my tea pot. And I'll eat off my drawing board. Things are always a little confused. I may be sorting out some writing or something and I can just leave the pages lying around, and if it's dinner time I can eat on top of them because I'm taking care of everything. Living alone has that advantage. Nobody moves anything. You can use your kitchen as a writing room. You can type on the stove.

Privacy is something I treasure. My home is like an island. I like to have people here but I like them to go after a while. I get a lot of visitors from back home, old friends who drop by and stay for a few days. Sometimes I find that very difficult because I'm under some sort of work pressure. Other times, it's really enjoyable. Only once has a person who stayed here really violated my space. I had to ask him to leave. Generally the people who stay here have been pretty understanding.

When I first came here, just for a short while, a woman lived with me. I still see her a lot. She's my closest friend. But I couldn't have her living here. I don't like anyone else living here, quite honestly. This is my treasured solitude space. I really have to have it.

I need this space because when I'm working really well, when I can do things and really get to places that I like to be, often very late at night, there's no one or nothing here that can interfere. There's just silence. And I don't feel any pressure to do anything else but work.

Something that's very interesting is that I learn a great deal about myself from my house, by trying to be incredibly conscious of what's going on here. Things have a really intense meaning for me. This place is very ritualized —where my gloves go, all sorts of things like that. It's not just keeping the key there because it's convenient, but I actually see it as a ritual. I try to be very aware of those sorts of things. I try to watch what I do as much as I can, sort of get out of myself, take a look at what I'm doing.

My house is really an extension of my

My house is really an extension of my whole self. The place and everything in it speaks back to me about how I am.

whole self. The place and everything in it speaks back to me about how I am. The way the towels are folded. I'm not finicky but I can tell by the stacks of my dishes what my mental state is. If I've washed them it means that I'm in a better state than if they're not washed. If everything is folded right and in its place, it means I'm together. The rightness is not a Germanic sense of order. If you look at my drawing stuff it looks like an incredible jumble. But every object that I use, every instrument, is located in a way that my hands can reach out without searching and get it. It's a very personal order; it's not necessarily neatness.

My friends are important to me. I have a lot of friends around work, some particularly close ones. I have a friend Jed with whom I work. We do projects together; we support each other; we give lectures together. And we share a lot in our work. We don't talk much really, because somehow each knows what the other's doing. That's fantastic.

Jed is like a rock in my life. I've never known him to be really down. Sometimes he's low in energy or something. But he never gets depressed. He's very proud and tough. He won't show a lot of his emotions. But he's just always there. That's important. The woman that he lives with is always around, too. We're all friends together. We do a lot of things together. We go to lectures at the school; we eat together a lot, and stuff like that. We cook. We have favorites that we cook for each other.

Most of my friends aren't married. Some of them live with people or some are married but live with other people. Apart from my parents, who have a model sort of marriage, I don't see

any "model marriages" among my friends. In fact, I often feel a little sorry for most of the married friends I have because they seem to be constrained.

I date fairly often. I have a friend Amy whom I go out with. We have a very good understanding. We don't make too many demands on each other. There's a certain amount of love. She has a lot of respect for my need for silence. She doesn't push. I really care a lot for her and I find it very good to be with her.

Then there are places in the city where I'll go if I just don't feel like seeing her. There are the coffee shops where I go. Sometimes I go there just to meet people. If I just hang around, I generally can meet people. Usually it's not difficult to meet women in bars or coffee shops. They're there for the same reason. Most often they'll be sitting there reading a book. I'll sit down and say, "Hi." The worst thing about meeting people is starting out. That's what puts me off. Sometimes I just feel here I am again, saying, "What's your name? What do you do?" There are also little games—"Do you want a light? Do you want a cigarette? Can I have a light?" That's why I smoke probably.

I pick out a woman I want to meet by looking for a certain softness. It's not purely aesthetic. It's a kind of intangible personality characteristic. Sometimes I'm wrong. I like stylish women. I don't like a lot of women that I see on the street. I don't really like women who wear combat boots and denims and have straggly hair. It seems to be fairly popular around here to have that image. But there are a lot of very beautiful women too. There's a woman, she's a psychologist, a very

I think people always are single;
you are born single.
You're always facing the world alone.

beautiful woman, that I met in the bank. I started a conversation with her because she attracted me so much, just because of the way she looked. She seemed so out of place here; I really thought she should be in New York or Paris. I spoke to her because she really looked so different. Those are the women who attract me, women who stand out from the denim thing.

There are a lot of ways of using sexual energy. A lot of the time I use my sexual energy for my work. I can go for a few weeks without getting bothered by not having sex. I don't need to have sex if I'm in a good working state.

Yet, at other times, I'll go hunting for sex, what I call "preying." It's sort of cyclical. But I know that I rechannel a lot of my sexual energy. And it doesn't particularly bother me although I don't know if it's healthy or unhealthy. A lot of my friends are in a similar situation.

One-night stands are all right, sometimes, I guess. I have had some good experiences. They're sort of exciting, but then I feel a little let down afterwards. Sometimes they turn out not to be one-nighters; sometimes they grow into relationships. I like risking that now and then. But I have to feel pretty much up for it. Sometimes I like one-night things because I'm free of any involvement the next morning. But when I think of my whole life I would not like to have to go hunting out one-night stands forever.

I don't think I'd like to be alone when I'm old. There are things even now that I don't like about being alone. Sometimes waking up in the morning is a little lonely. And coming home to this place just like I left it can be lonely. No one's moved anything. Sometimes that's nice and sometimes it's not.

The other day I went out. It was a very windy day. While I was gone a window blew open and the wind came to visit me. It moved everything around. I came home and the wind had been here. I like coming home to surprises, and you don't often get that when you live alone.

There are certain times when I just want somebody around. I don't think it's ever from a deep feeling of loneliness. It's just that there are odd moments when it would be nice to share something—like when I've discovered something incredibly exciting at three o'clock in the morning, and I'm dancing around. Sometimes I get that sort of energy that I can't let out because there isn't anyone nearby. Moments like that I would like to share with people. Sometimes when I come home and I've had a weird day at school or something, and I want to talk to someone, it would be nice just to have somebody around. And it would be nice to have somebody to do my laundry; I'll tell you the truth—I hate doing laundry.

But in the balance, for right now, I want to remain single. I think people always are single; you are born single. You're always facing the world alone.

Part II Skills

Being Single

Voices

MAKING THE CHOICE

I have never met a person who has over-powered me or impressed me or awed me, stunned me enough to say, "This is it. I'm throwing in my fate with someone else."

The biggest advantage of getting married would be having someone to share my interests, energy, and abilities with. Learning about this person and from her would help me become more aware of myself.

On the other hand, there's a lot I'd have to give up. There's my total selfishness. I now can do what I want, when I want, where I want, with whom I want, how I want. I have to consult with no one. I do totally what I want to do. I have married friends who have to worry about time, children, their partner's views, society. I wouldn't like that. I'm thriving now on my sense of freedom.

George P., age 25

When I was younger I had a chance to look at the lives of my friends who had gotten married. It wasn't a life style that I envied. They all had babies within the first year or two. I will admit that I was never terribly attracted to the idea of having a lot of little kids in diapers. I was never very patient with kids and I could sense I wouldn't have been a very good mother of small children. And then, too, they were struggling financially for the most part and living in cramped quarters. So I didn't see things that made me want to get married.

Lynn H., age 45

The driving force behind my wanting to solve this problem of living alone comes from books I've read that indicate man's ultimate problem is to live with himself. When he's learned how to live with himself, then he can live with other people.

Jeff P., married 22 years,
divorced 3 years, age 47

Raised as a Catholic, I had a very difficult time relating to sex. Raised as a snob, I had a difficult time accepting anyone who was not "good enough." Constant moves during my teens and college made long-term relationships difficult to establish. I did have a number of proposals but turned them down because I probably never really wanted to get married. It was never a conscious choice. It just happened.

Ruth G., age 46

I know of only one or two marriages that I would want to have. So, when I'm lying in bed feeling sorry for myself that there's nobody lying next to me holding me, I say to myself, "O.K. now, think about the marriages of your friends and what they're getting out of their relationships." And I know I don't want what they have. I would really choose my present single life.

Sara C., age 31

I think I'm beginning to see being single as a positive life style and a growth experience, whereas before I saw it as a temporary state. Now, I don't think of it as either permanent or temporary. I just think it *is* and I see it as a rich time in my life that may last forever or may not. I don't feel locked into it. I feel very posi-

tive about it. I feel like it will probably end if it's right for it to end. Or it won't. I can accept it either way.

Donna R., married 2 years,
divorced 7 years, age 30

I don't know if my singleness is temporary or permanent. The longer it goes on, the more I think it's going to be permanent because the less likely I am to make compromises. I work very hard on the quality of my life. I've made a

lot of money. I've got everything together. The main reason I wanted to remarry was to have more children. I always imagined having four or six children. But I'm getting too old for that.

Jennifer F., married 5 years,
divorced 5 years, age 34

I don't want to get remarried. I think I won the first time and I just wouldn't want to run the risk again. I don't have to get married. I can get along. Of course, I miss having somebody love me and care for me. But you get adjusted to things.

Eleanor M., married 32 years, widowed 10 years, age 73

I'll probably try living with a woman but not getting married. There's a psychological difference. I suppose it's something in my head. I just think there's the hassle of being married, of getting out of it, even though it's easier than it was. Certainly there's a financial hassle. I can't think of any reason for getting married again unless I want to have kids.

Patrick R., married 4 years, divorced 2 years, age 34

I know there are problems in being married but they don't frighten me. The kinds of problems I have right now are not very real. Going out with women, getting a date, sleeping with somebody. It's all so transitory. After you do that, what have you got anyway? When you have a permanent relationship you have something that's really worth working for. Like if you have kids you're dealing with how their lives will come out. That's a very important thing. I'm not doing anything important right now.

Jesse F., age 34

It may be the way I was brought up or society. Who the hell knows? But I've always had the feeling that I am going to get married and live happily ever after. I think it's a fantasy that most other single people still believe—that we're going to meet that right person.

Tom E., age 30

HOW OTHERS SEE YOU

My relatives are very upset that I am single. They don't understand it at all. I think they feel sorry for me. For a while there was always the question, "So, what's new on the social front?" And I always felt bad that I couldn't meet their expectations.

Some of my friends, too, feel responsible for fixing me up. When I was living off in the country, they felt, "Oh, how sad. It's such a reclusive place. You'll never meet anybody."

But some people who know me better seem to accept my singleness and don't seem to question it. I mean, they may want to know about it—to know what I feel—but they're not judgmental. At one point I had friends who would drop in on the spur of the moment just to see what I did at night. (You wonder why a single person feels really weird.) I'm not the sort of person who loves to be interrupted at night. But they would do this intentionally—suddenly pop in and look around really fast to see if maybe I had elves in the house. They'd find me just sitting there.

There was one friend in particular. He had an entirely different life style from mine. He was living alone, too, but not by any personal desire. He was really a social butterfly. He would arrange his life so that every night he was busy. And just as I could not stand his life or really understand why he had to schedule every free moment, he could not understand how I could go for weeks without filling my evenings, at least having dinner with somebody. So I think he thought that something must be going on in my house that he ought to know about.

Donna R., married 2 years, divorced 7 years, age 30

I have some married friends who have been coupled almost since they left their parents' homes. And they say they wish they could have their own space to do what they want without compromise. They wish they could buy things without having to justify them. They feel that their husbands and their children come first. My self-indulgence is very appealing to them. I mean, I only have me to take care of. They eat their hearts out looking at my life, especially when they have an aggravation at home. They drop in at my house and it looks wonderful to them.

They really have an unreal view of my life. They don't realize that I have to do it all. I have to take the garbage out *every* time. I have to wash the sink *every* time. I have to change *every* light bulb, I have to pay *every* bill, I have to pick up *every* single thing that I mess up. I do every dish. I clean the refrigerator every time. I do it all. I hate doing it all. My married friends see my life as the ultimate freedom. And it is. But it's also the ultimate responsibility, and they forget that part.

Sara C., age 31

I always thought I'd get married, but now that I'm not I wonder what people think about me. Here I am, 34 and not married. Will they feel sorry for me? I don't feel sorry for myself. I'm not talking about people who know me because my friends know that not being married is part of the way I live, part of my ideology. But people who look at my résumé or something. They just see the statistics of my life. And they'll think, "Oh, God, poor guy. He's not married. Wonder what's wrong with him."

Jesse F., age 34

JOYS OF THE SINGLE LIFE

Living alone has helped me to get in touch with me. I've learned to like my own company. There's a certain completeness about it. I have a wonderful sense of "I'm O.K."

Sara C., age 31

I like living my own life the way I want to. And I don't have to consider all the vagaries that men bring into the situation.

Ellen B., married 22 years,
divorced 3 years, age 58

It's an incredible feeling of self-indulgence, of liberty, of freedom to move, of being able to do what I want. I make the decisions. I can fit everything I own into my car. I can say good-bye to a job and take off for some new life. The possibilities that that presents to my mind are overwhelming. That awes me. Sometimes I become totally amazed by the incredible potential.

George P., age 25

I like having my own space for a change. And having the opportunity to come to know myself and to really be myself rather than being what other people expect me to be .

Bruce F., married 10 years,
separated 2 years, age 38

What I like best is the freedom. I can take the job I want. I can work the hours I want. I can live where I want.

Max F., age 29

I enjoy my independence. I'm probably one of the few people that really likes to be alone. I enjoy doing things on my own, having my own schedule. I keep fairly erratic hours. I'm up late at night and sometimes I'll sleep until ten o'clock in the morning. I like this flexibility. I guess I'm selfish about myself. I'm self-centered. I just don't enjoy working on somebody else's schedule. I like to be able to pick up and go somewhere if I want to or do whatever I want to when I want to do it.

Patrick R., married 4 years,
divorced 2 years, age 34

Alone

COLETTE

As always, I give a great sigh when I close the door of my ground-floor flat behind me. Is it a sigh of weariness, or relaxation, or relief? Or does it spring from the bitterness of solitude? Better not think of it, far better not!

But what on earth is the matter with me tonight? It must be this icy December fog, like particles of frost hanging in the air, quivering in an iridescent halo round the gas lamps and melting on one's lips with a taste of creosote. And besides, this new quarter where I live, looming up all white behind Les Ternes, is enough to discourage both one's eyes and one's spirit.

My street, under the greenish gas at this hour, is a morass of toffee-like, creamy mud—coffee-coloured, maroon and caramel yellow—a sort of crumbling, slushy trifle in which the floating bits of meringue are lumps of concrete. Even my house, the only one on the street, has a sort of "it can't be true" look. But its new walls and thin partitions offer, at a modest rent, a shelter sufficiently comfortable for "ladies on their own" like me.

When you are a "lady on your own," in other words the landlord's abomination, outcast and terror all rolled into one, you take what you find, lodge where you may and put up with newly plastered walls.

The house where I live compassionately shelters quite a colony of "ladies on their own." On the mezzanine floor we have the acknowledged mistress of Young, of Young-Automobiles; above, the girl-friend, very much "kept," of the Comte de Bravailles; higher up are two fair-haired sisters, both of whom are visited every day by the same man, a very-correct-gentleman-in-industry; higher still a terrible little tart makes as much of a

racket night and day as an unleashed fox-terrier, screaming, playing the piano, singing and throwing empty bottles out of the window.

"She's a disgrace to the house," Madame Young-Automobiles said one day.

Finally, on the ground floor, there is myself who neither screams, nor plays the piano, nor ever receives gentlemen and still less ladies. The little tart on the fourth floor makes too much noise and I not enough, as the concierge does not fail to remark to me. "It's funny, one never knows whether Madame is there because one doesn't hear her. One would never think she was an artiste!"

What an ugly December night it is! The radiator smells of iodoform, Blandine has forgotten to put my hot-water bottle in my bed, and even my dog is in a bad mood. Grumpy and shivering, she merely casts one black and white glance at me, without leaving her basket. I must say! I don't expect triumphal arches and illuminations, but all the same . . .

No need to search the place, to peer in the corners or look under the bed, there is no one here, no one but myself. What I see in the big looking-glass in my bedroom is no longer the painted image of an itinerant music-hall artiste. It reflects only—myself.

Behold me then, just as I am! This evening I shall not be able to escape the meeting in the long mirror, the soliloquy which I have a hundred times avoided, accepted, fled from, taken up again and broken off. I feel in advance, alas, the uselessness of trying to change the subject. This evening I shall not feel sleepy, and the spell of a book—even a brand-new book with that smell of printers' ink and paper fresh from the press that makes

There are days when solitude, for someone of my age, is a heady wine which intoxicates you with freedom.

you think of coal and trains and departures—even that spell will not be able to distract me from myself.

Behold me then, just as I am. Alone alone, and for the rest of my life, no doubt. Already alone; it's early for that. When I turned thirty I did not feel cast down because mine is a face that depends on the expression which animates it, the colour of my eyes, and the defiant smile that plays over it—what Marinetti calls my *gaiezza volpina*. But if I look like a fox, it's a fox without guile, which a hen could catch! And a fox without rapacity, one that remembers only the trap and the cage. A gay-looking fox, if you like, but only because the corners of its mouth and eyes look as if they were smiling.

It is true enough that I do look like a fox. But a slender, pretty fox is not an ugly thing, is it? Brague says too that I look like a rat when I purse my lips and blink my eyelids so as to see better. I see nothing to mind in that. . . .

It is one o'clock already. What am I waiting for? A smart little lash with the whip to make the obstinate creature go on again. But no one will give it me because . . . because I am alone. How clearly one sees, in that long frame which holds my reflection, that I'm used already to living alone!

No matter what visitor, for a mere tradesman, or even for my charwoman Blandine, I should raise this drooping neck, straighten that slouching hip and clasp those empty hands. But tonight I am so alone.

Alone! Indeed one might think I was pitying myself for it!

"If you live all alone," said Brague, "it's because you really want to, isn't it?"

Certainly I "really" want to, and in fact I *want* to, quite simply. Only, well . . . there are days when solitude, for someone of my age, is a heady wine which intoxicates you with freedom, others when it is a bitter tonic, and still others when it is a poison which makes you beat your head against the wall.

This evening I would much prefer not to say which it is; all I want is to remain undecided, and not to be able to say whether the shiver which will seize me when I slip between the cold sheets comes from fear or contentment.

Alone . . . and for a long time past. The proof is that I am giving way to the habit of talking to myself and of holding conversations with my dog, and the fire, and my own reflection. It is an idiosyncrasy which recluses and old prisoners fall into; but I'm not like them, I'm free. And if I talk to myself it is because I have a writer's need to express my thoughts in rhythmical language.

Facing me from the other side of the looking-glass, in that mysterious reflected room, is the image of "a woman of letters who has turned out badly." They also say of me that I'm "on the stage," but they never call me an actress. Why? The nuance is subtle, but there is certainly a polite refusal, on the part both of the public and my friends themselves, to accord me any standing in this career which I have nevertheless adopted. A woman of letters who has turned out badly: that is what I must remain for everyone, I who no longer write, who deny myself the pleasure, the luxury of writing.

From *The Vagabond* by Colette

Books

SINGLE

by Peter J. Stein
Prentice-Hall, Inc., 1976

Crammed with facts and figures, *Single* is a fascinating hour or two's worth of sociological reading.

Did you know that:

There are more than 47 million single, separated, divorced and widowed people over the age of 18 in the United States?

There is an identifiable "singles industry" in the U.S., comprising singles' bars, singles' resorts, singles' clubs, singles' housing, that does $40 billion a year in business?

Not only has the divorce rate risen dramatically, but the number of people remaining single is increasing dramatically as well and that divorced people are choosing to remain single in ever-growing numbers?

Only two percent of executives in fifty major corporations surveyed were single?

Among the issues that Stein attends to are "The Single and Society," "Single Adults and their Parents," "Sex and Singles," "Sources of Support for Singles," "The Future of Singles in America." He presents the results of surveys, studies, and interviews in a crisp, readable narrative and packs scads of interesting information into a small space.

SINGLE BLESSEDNESS

by Margaret Adams
Basic Books, Inc., 1976

Single Blessedness is a frontal attack on the still widely held notion that there is "something wrong" with the person who chooses to remain uncoupled in this paired-up country.

Margaret Adams examines the strong bias against singles in today's society as well as in past societies. She confronts psychological descriptions of the "singles pathology," revealing them to be less scientific and more cultural wishful thinking, and argues that there is ample evidence to demonstrate that many singles choose their life style not because they are emotionally immature or because there is a paucity of potential mates, but because they value personal autonomy so highly they are unwilling to make the compromises successful marriage demands.

While seeking to undercut society's distorted attitude toward singles, Adams also works to help establish a positive identity context into which singles can fit themselves. She celebrates the joys of singleness through recounting her own experiences and the experiences of many others she interviewed. They all speak of the spaciousness, the mobility, the creativity their lives allow them.

Adams has written a polemic more than a study, and often her arguments smack of "singles chauvinism." Despite prose that is cold and difficult, this book is the kind of "give-'em-hell" statement that many singles will be happy to rally around.

NAKED NOMADS: UNMARRIED MEN IN AMERICA

by George Gilder
Quadrangle, 1975

George Gilder paints a bleak picture of single men's lives. To start, he gathers an array of statistics and studies that show how bad off single men in America are. For instance: "Between the ages of forty-five and fifty-four, for example, single white men with college de-

THE CHOICE TO BE SINGLE

Table VIII

Pushes and Pulls Toward Being Married and Being Single

Toward Being Married

Pushes (negatives in present situation)	*Pulls (attractions in potential situations)*
Pressure from parents	Approval of parents
Need to leave home	Desire for family
Fear of independence	Example of peers
Loneliness	Romanticization of marriage
Cultural expectations, socialization	Physical attraction
	Emotional attachment and love

Toward Being Single

Pushes	*Pulls*
Restrictions within relationship: Suffocating one-to-one relationship, feeling trapped	Career opportunities
Obstacles to self-development	Variety of experiences and plurality of roles
Boredom, unhappiness, and anger	Self-sufficiency
Role playing and conformity to expectations	Sexual availability
	Exciting life style
	Freedom to change and mobility
	Sustaining friendships

The strength of these pushes and pulls is highly relative. They vary in intensity according to a number of factors. Pressures from parents to marry may be experienced very strongly by some and hardly at all by others. Some see being alone with great fear, and they seek a mate to fill the perceived void. Others seek friends with whom to spend time. Physical attraction and emotional involvement can lead to marriage for some, to living together for others, or can be enjoyed without a more permanent attachment by still others. However, the same person experiences the same pushes or pulls in different ways at different stages of his or her life cycle. There is a roughly defined set of age categories that helps shape people's relations to one another. People expect different accomplishments and are prepared to accept different behavior according to their age group (Turner, 1970:370). Philip Slater (1970), Margaret Mead, (1970), Richard Flacks (1971) and others have documented the confusing and contradictory elements in the transition from adolescence to adulthood in American society. With respect to marriage, however, there is a clear cultural imperative to marry in one's late teens or early twenties, although with an increase in the number of high school graduates going on to college, and with more women working, the age of first marriage has risen. While the marriage imperative is stronger for women, men are also expected to marry.

From Single

63

grees earn an average of about $10,500. Married men earn about $19,000 . . . single men are far more prone to mental and physical disorders than any other large group of Americans, with the possible exception of the divorced."

Gilder uses the surveys, the studies, and the statistics, along with his own personal experiences as a single man, as grist for serious and difficult ruminations on maleness, sexual liberation, social unrest, the inner life, and relations between men and women. His reasoning is acute; his arguments demand serious attention; he is sometimes quite daring in opposing conventional cant; and he is never trivial. You may not agree with him when he writes "[a man] is optional. One man can impregnate a hundred women, but only one woman can bear a man's child and acknowledge his paternity. Even then the probation continues, since usually, if there is an extreme conflict, the woman can take away the child. It is what the man does, how he performs, what he provides that overcome his biological dispensibility." But even if you don't agree with him you can't dismiss him as some silly sophomore. This is a serious book that should be read by serious observers of the modern scene.

SINGLE WOMEN, ALONE AND TOGETHER

by Lucia H. Bequaert
The Beacon Press, 1976

Single Women, Alone and Together is a sound and thorough study of the condition of single women in American society today. Beyond that it is an encouragement for single women to live positive, productive lives on their own and support each other rather than cop out to the pressure to couple in order to "give their lives meaning."

Interspersed among the sections on sociology and interpretation and analysis are the voices of single women speaking about their lives and the issues that concern them. One rhapsodizes about the spaciousness she feels in her life alone. A middle-aged, never-married woman speaks of the joys of becoming part of a family by adopting a daughter. Two young women talk about the difficulty of breaking away from the expectations laid on them by their parents. The difficulties of finding dignified work and supporting her three children concern a 34-year-old divorced mother. A divorced Catholic woman relates how hard it is to get the church to respond humanely to her needs. Another middle-aged divorced woman speaks in tough, realistic terms about the hardships of being the breadwinner for herself and her daughters.

Bequaert's book combines sociological data, reasoned analysis, and stories from women's lives to present a careful and thoughtful look at single women.

THE WOMAN ALONE

by Patricia O'Brien
Quadrangle, 1973

Patricia O'Brien took two years off from her family—a husband and four daughters—to live alone in another city and visit on weekends. This book blends her experiences, the experiences of other women alone, and her reflections in a strong and tender statement about the need women have to be alone so they might experience themselves as whole persons.

The Woman Alone is not a tract. Though not as downright poetical as Anne Lindbergh's *Gift from the Sea*, its quiet, sometimes almost lyrical tones have more in common with that book than with polemical political ones.

Among the many lenses through which O'Brien views the actualities and possibilities of women alone are: "The Woman Alone Through History," an interesting account of single women from Hawthorne's Hester Prynne through Ibsen's Nora to Helen Gurley Brown's "Single Girl"; "Youth and Age," comparisons and contrasts of the state of single women at various ages—Tina is a Playboy Bunny who "has it made," Barbara is a middle-aged, never-married English professor; "Power and Powerlessness," a look at the traditional ways women have wielded power—chiefly through manipulation—and some searching questions about the proper ways and means of power.

It isn't O'Brien's intention to provide conclusions or solutions: "This is a personal book; a question book not an answer book; a search, not a discovery." She asks her questions in such a warm and human way that we all can identify with her.

THE CHALLENGE
OF BEING SINGLE

by Marie Edwards and Eleanor Hoover
J.P. Tarcher, Inc., 1974

The Challenge of Being Single grew out of workshops in which singles worked to jettison all that cultural baggage that identifies the unpaired as the unhappy, the undesirable, the unfit. Singles shared the difficulties of being single, and the joys. It was definitely the positive that was accentuated, though the negative wasn't eliminated. On the minus side—tax laws, restaurants, personnel directors all favor the married. On the plus side, singles spoke of being free to go where they wanted to when they wanted to, of not having to be "on" for anyone at the end of the day, of not having to negotiate how they'd spend an evening, money, vacations.

There are plenty of hints in this book for handling situations that often cause problems for single people—traveling alone, eating out alone, having couple friends, platonic relationships, dealing with loneliness. But the book's real service is as a morale booster. Single people who take its message to heart will come away with a more positive sense of themselves as unpaired members of society.

A LIFE OF YOUR OWN

by Harriet LaBarre
David McKay Company, Inc., 1972

And now for a chipper, optimistic, bright-eyed-and-bushy-tailed book about how neat it can be to live alone. Harriet LaBarre comes on like a cheery next-door neighbor brimming with all sorts of advice for the single woman.

First off, she says, you've got to have the right attitude. Think of yourself as beautifully alone, not lonely. Then, get a job to add some structure, some *backbone*, to your life, so you won't just sit around all the time feeling sorry for yourself.

Next, start learning about how to handle money. Live where you really want to and spend time and energy making your home environment one that truly pleases you. Have parties. Travel. Make nice, attractive meals for yourself. Have happy and tender love affairs. In short, live it up.

LaBarre deals mostly with surfaces; she never penetrates to the core of the issues, so this isn't a book you'd read to stimulate some deep meditations on the state of living alone. But if you're after a breezy, chatty, "up" kind of pep talk, you might like to try *A Life of Your Own*.

Companionship

Voices

FRIENDSHIP

I use my friends for all the things that married people use their spouses for. I have wonderful friends. I'm close to them. I see them all the time. Three are married women. Three are platonic male friends I've known for between 10 and 15 years. Even though they all live nearby, some of them I write letters to regularly because we like to record our friendships and what's going on in our heads.

Jennifer F., married 5 years,
divorced 5 years, age 34

I have one particular friend who I'm very close to. I love her. And she would always help me out if I needed it, like meeting me at the airport, or if I were sick, or if I were involved in an accident. Any kind of disastrous thing. I know some single people feel isolated in that they don't have one particular person they can call on in an emergency, the way a married person can always call on a mate. But I don't feel that at all because of my one particular friend.

Lynn H., age 45

I use my friends primarily as shrinks. I think I'd be very frustrated if I didn't have people to talk to. That aspect is more important to me than the social activity.

Martha A., married 10 years,
divorced 5 years, age 37

Friends are not terribly important in my life. I have a lot of acquaintances but not many good friends. It's partly because I've moved a lot and also because I travel so much. But I'm very happy to be by myself, reading or watching television or whatever. I guess the most social thing I do is play ball with some regulars.

Patrick R., married 4 years,
divorced 2 years, age 34

I think it's important to see your friends just about every day. That makes them part of your family. So many people are busy, it's hard to be in sync with them. It's hard to share your life with them.

Jesse F., age 34

I take whatever each person has got to give me. Some people are intellectual friends. Some are emotional friends. Some are "doing-with" friends. So I have different friends for different things.

Sally A., age 33

I think friends are more important to single people than to people in couples, because when you're single and you need a friend, you *really* need a friend. A friend is somebody you can impose on, with license, and that has to be established. But much as that's a need for me, I still have a problem finding that kind of friend. I'm so worried about what other people will feel that I won't ask for what I need, unless I'm in pain. So my friends don't realize how important they are to me, especially when they are in couples. My couple friends can turn to each other in an emergency whereas I have no one to turn to. There have been times in my life when I've had a very bad emotional experience and just really needed somebody. And those are times usually when

I don't worry about whether or not I'm going to burden these people. I just know I have to burden them and I hope that they can take it.

Donna R., married 2 years,
divorced 7 years, age 30

CHOOSING FRIENDS

My best friends are about ten years younger than I am. I like that because they tend to be a lot less conservative than people my age, and

it's really opened my eyes. I don't feel older than they are when I'm with them. In some ways I seem younger because I'm less experienced.

Martha A., married 10 years,
divorced 5 years, age 37

In general I find that single friends are more available to me. They understand my demands better. I know they might need me in the same way I might need them. There's more reciprocity. I feel it's more demanding when I turn to someone in a couple. It's more difficult. So I try to find people who are single.

But I do have couple friends, and when I got divorced they did not drop me. It wasn't like my mother's experience when my father died. She was gradually phased out of friendships. I was just ten years old but I saw her long-time friendships go down the drain. I felt enormously sorry for my mother. I'm sure that had an impact on me. When I got divorced I made a conscious attempt not to spread my gloom to my married friends. I felt that perhaps their relationships were no more stable than my own had been. And I really got messages from them that it wasn't a good idea to bring the doom in.

Donna R., married 2 years,
divorced 7 years, age 30

As I get older I find it more and more difficult to have close friends, mainly because I have grown so far ahead of them professionally. It's difficult to find someone single in my age range, in my money range, and in my business range. I find this sad and one of the most difficult things to handle

Ruth G., age 46

One thing that happened when I went through getting separated was not relating to people as couples any more. That means if I have a friend who has a boy friend, I'm not necessarily going to try to get as close to him as I am to her. The importance of the relationship is with one person. One benefit of this is that when couples I know split up, I don't go through the thing of having to side with one of them. I can continue to see both of them separately.

Larry H., married 4 years,
separated 2 years, age 32

I feel I can be a bit more decadent with single friends. We can indulge ourselves more, be a bit more foolish, more carefree with our time, our money, our thoughts. At the same time,

there are some married people who are incredibly important to me. I'll invite couples over or go out with them. I'm happy to make up a threesome.

George P., age 25

PLATONIC FRIENDS

Platonic friends are the great strength of my life. When I was married I was close to a lot of men. I was one of the boys. After the divorce I didn't get involved with these men because we had a kind of incest taboo. We'd been like brothers and sister for so long.

I also have platonic friends who are former lovers. I'm very close to every man I've ever gone to bed with. There aren't any that have gone out of my life. I've never gone back to bed with anybody once it was over—never "for old time's sake." But I have a close, loving relationship with everyone I've ever been physically intimate with.

And then I have some male friends who are platonic friends simply because they're too young. I tell them it would be like me committing statutory rape.

Jennifer F., married 5 years,
divorced 5 years, age 34

I have some very close male friends who are married. There certainly are temptations but once those are overcome, platonic friendships can be maintained and they mean a great deal.

Ruth G., age 46

So many of the men I've known have died that most of my friends are female, although I like men. I like to talk to men. I would like platonic friendships, but around here the widowers would be afraid you were after them.

Eleanor M., married 32 years,
widowed 10 years, age 73

There have been times when close women friends and I have become sexually involved.

But if the groundwork for a good friendship was there to start, after the sexual involvement is over we are still close friends.

George P., age 25

PETS AND THINGS

It never occurred to me to have a dog until four years ago when a fellow I knew had to get rid of his. I took her. At first I didn't know what to expect. I saw a terrific responsibility and I was afraid I wouldn't be able to handle it. But it is worth it. I get love. I get the steadiest, almost perfect kind of love you can imagine. She's always there when I come home. She provides exercise for me. She never challenges me or talks back when I talk to her. And I talk to her all the time. That's the classic idea of the old maid, isn't it? But I have a feeling that everybody talks to their pets.

Lynn H., age 45

Books have always been a great source of companionship to me. People in books are often more real to me than people in real life.

Karl C., married twice, divorced 10 years, age 68

FAMILY

There are five of us—three brothers and a sister. And we're all fairly close. I enjoy seeing them. We were together Thanksgiving time. It was so refreshing for me to go up there and spend three days with them. All my depressions and all my problems were gone.

We get together for all the holidays and usually for everybody's birthday. It's nice because my sister has five kids and one of my brothers has one, so I get to be around little kids. I get to be a nice aunt. Then I get to go home and they keep the kids.

Holly H., married 3 years, divorced 3 years, age 29

I spend a few weeks with my mother every summer. I never could get along with her until about six years ago, and then I finally got to the point where I could stay with her. Now we get along fine. It's a very satisfying feeling to finally make friends with her.

Ellen B., married 22 years, divorced 3 years, age 58

I get a lot of support from my parents. They've even loaned me money to help me pay some of the debts caused by my separation. But the best thing is they keep telling me I'm doing a good job with my kids, and that kind of stuff.

Bruce F., married 10 years, separated 2 years, age 38

My son has been wonderful to me. But neither of us is dependent on the other. He has done all kinds of wonderful things for me. But there will be three or four weeks that I don't even see him or hear from him. That's the way it should be, I think. He knows that I am independent and I can get along.

Eleanor M., married 32 years, widowed 10 years, age 73

My family is important to me in that I do believe I have a special responsibility to support them and to aid them. But I don't go out of my way to spend time with them. Friends really fulfill more of my needs than my family does.

George P., age 25

Family

GAIL GODWIN

On an impulse, Jane decided to sacrifice her planned reticence over Edith for the further success of this lunch. Edith would not mind. In fact, if she were able to know, she would probably prefer having her death discussed. She had discussed it herself so often, as if she were planning for it, like a future vacation.

"Actually, I have to go South. My grandmother died early this morning. I'm leaving on the evening plane."

"Oh, I'm sorry! Was she very old? Has she been sick for a long time?"

Jane could see Edith through Sonia's eyes: a "grandmother."

"No. I think parts of her were wearing out. Her back gave her trouble. But when the doctor x-rayed it, he said the spine was simply disintegrating and there was nothing he could do. He said, 'What do you expect, at your age,' and she changed doctors. The new doctor, it seems, put her into a small private hospital to see if rest would improve it. She died there—quite painlessly, my mother said. Almost like taking the next breath."

"How old was she?"

"Well, I figured it up once. She was eighty-six. But she would have been furious if I ever let on that I knew."

"Was she one of those traditional Southern belles?" asked Sonia.

"Oh, Lord, yes," said Jane, beginning to get animated over the prospect of what Gerda would call "mythmaking about your family." "Edith—we all called her Edith—was the perfect Southern lady. She was elegant, snobbish, beautiful to the very end. Her skin—and I'm not exaggerating—when I saw her this past Christmas was smoother than mine. She took exquisite care of herself. She was a woman who was always in style. I'll tell you a strange story. It just came to me. When I went home this Christmas, Kitty—that's my mother—and I went to take Edith to the new doctor, for her back. When we arrived at her apartment, she was sitting very straight in her armchair. She had put up her hair by herself, though we came early especially so we could help her with it. She had her make-up on, her diamond earrings screwed through her ears, her silk blouse, her little diamond brooch, her slip, her stockings, her shoes, and all of her rings. Her face had odd little spots of color in each cheek though she is normally very pale. She prides herself—I mean prided herself—on this pallor.

"Now she looked as though she were blushing for shame. As if something had embarrassed her greatly. She looked at us both rather coldly, as if she had forgotten exactly who we were—these two women who had walked into her apartment. Then she said, rather haughtily, 'I don't think I'll be able to go to that doctor. I haven't the strength to put on my skirt, you see. Kitty, will you please call and cancel the appointment?'

"While Kitty was on the phone, talking to the receptionist, Edith motioned me closer. 'Do you know what happened this morning, Jane? I saw the awfulest thing while I was sitting in front of that mirror getting ready.' I could see her reflection and mine in her triple mirror. It's one of those old-fashioned things with drawers on each side. The three of us have watched ourselves grow older in these funny mirrors. Those mirrors are the only ones I know that show you how you used to look, how you look now, and how you're going to look.

"I asked Edith what she had seen. I had no

Those mirrors are the only ones I know that
show you how you used to look, how you look now,
and how you're going to look.

idea what she would reply, she looked so strange. I have never seen her look so . . . chastened. 'Well,' she said very softly, leaning toward me, 'I saw this . . . I saw this *tired little old lady*, that's what I saw.' And I've just realized this, Sonia, talking to you: Edith had made up her mind that morning she was going to die. She had died to herself, to her image of herself. It was now only a matter of finding an excuse to justify her death to us."

"Ah," said Sonia significantly. She drank more wine. "Yes."

Jane was gratified. She knew she had found an audience who appreciated the shape of this story, grasped its symbols and implications.

"Do you have any sisters or brothers?"

"Two half-brothers and a half-sister. Much younger. The boys are thirteen and sixteen and Emily is nineteen. She's in law school. She got married at fifteen."

"You're kidding."

"No. She's a unique person, all right. I don't think she likes me very much. I think she thinks I have too many problems when life, according to her, has been so simple. I am sure she feels herself, secretly, to be the older sister. I have never known her to be a real child." That's quite enough, thought Jane. No more family myths. We'll have a few moments of awkward silence and soup-slurping.

But Sonia said, "How do you mean? Tell me about her. I'm fascinated."

"Well, to begin with, she decided she wanted this boy who is now her husband when she was twelve years old. He was eighteen at the time. A very shy, isolated boy, the son of one of my mother's best friends, a woman who had died very suddenly and tragi-

cally. Kitty often had John—that's the boy—and his father to dinner. Emily decided she wanted to marry John one day, and went to work."

"Oh, I want to hear this. How did she go to work? What do you mean by that: *going to work?*" Sonia's dark eyes snapped with lively interest and Jane knew she was spellbound.

Yes, that is the story we still love most, she thought. How some woman went to work and got her man. Even "emancipated women" like Sonia love to hear the old, old story one more time.

So Jane launched into the story of how Emily Sparks, age twelve, had looked across the roast beef and potatoes at this shy young man and begun her campaign to annex him to her life. Jane described the fierce Ping-Pong matches in the basement after dinner. "She would rip her best dresses to pieces under the arms to win her point." And the elaborate table settings, the candlelight, the poring over *The Joy of Cooking* to get it right. "Even at twelve, Emily was an excellent cook, the best in the family, much better than Kitty, because she could organize things and she never got ruffled and she chopped all her onions and things ahead of time—that kind of thing. Emily would say, 'Kitty, can we have John and his daddy to dinner on Saturday?' and Kitty would say, 'Oh, no, Emily, we just had them and I don't feel like cooking a great big feast.' '*I'll* do everything—if you ask them,' Emily would say, and Kitty, who loathes cooking, fell for the bribe every time. . . ."

"I love this story," said Sonia. "May I pour myself some more wine? Here, let me pour you some, too."

From *The Odd Woman* by Gail Godwin

Books

COMMUNES, LAW AND COMMONSENSE: A LEGAL MANUAL FOR COMMUNITIES

by Lee Goldstein
New Community Projects, 1974

Here's a thoroughgoing manual for those interested in setting up communes. In many, if not most, cases, making a commune happen isn't so simple as just finding a bunch of folks who want to live together. The law tends to look unfavorably on communes. For instance, many, many communities have laws forbidding more than a certain number (often two or three) of unrelated people from living together in a "single-family" dwelling. People who want to set up an out-in-the-open, legitimate commune may find themselves ensnarled in a net of legal difficulties. Before paying $50 per hour for a lawyer after you're already in trouble with local officials, it might be a good idea to spend three bucks on this book and try to anticipate and circumvent the difficulties that can arise.

Communes, Law and Commonsense covers a lot of legal territory: "Communes, Law and the Constitution"; "Morality Laws"; "Self-Defense (What to do When the 'Man' Comes Knocking)"; "Peoples Associations (Forms of Organization and Real Estate Transactions)"; and "Zoning and Building Codes." There is ample documentation, including excerpts from crucial legal decisions. And an excellent appendix with tables listing morality statutes by state, forms of organization by state, and examples of zoning laws.

All in all, *Communes, Law and Commonsense* is a practical and valuable book for those really serious about wanting to create a communal life style as an alternative to the nuclear-family style that prevails in today's America.

THE NEW COMMUNES

by Ron E. Roberts
Prentice-Hall, Inc., 1971

The move to a communal life style is a vigorous, if tiny, movement in America today. For singles, a communal life offers the advantage of providing a built-in family without the traditional nuclear-family configuration.

The New Communes is a good primer on the commune scene in America, past and present. Ron Roberts takes a look at early communal societies in the New World—Shakers, Rappites, Mennonites, the New Harmony community, the Oneida community, and others. He traces the antecedents of many of today's communal movements to the Beat Generation, and to political and civil-rights activists. He examines the characteristics of communal societies—why they are formed, who the members are, how they govern themselves, how they stay together. And he sketches various present-day communal groups—"Erotic Utopias," or communes built on a nontraditional approach to sexual relationships, "Hip Communes" such as Morningstar Ranch and Tolstoy Farm, religious communities, radical political ones, and Twin Oaks, a community based on B.F. Skinner's *Walden Two*.

This book isn't intended to be a study in depth; it is a sound, interesting, readable survey. It is certainly worthwhile for those interested in the history and present state of communizing; and it will likely be helpful for those bent on pursuing communal living as an

COMMUNAL EXPERIMENTATION—GROUP MARRIAGE

How much sexual repression or control is necessary for a communal society to exist? Some communal advocates of group marriage believe they have found the key to this question. "Group marriage," writes one communalist, ". . . avoids the pitfalls of exclusive monogamy and impersonalistic promiscuity."[1] Does group marriage in fact avoid the pitfalls of monogamy and unrestrained sex? To answer this question it is important to remember that current experimenters in group marriage have grown to adulthood in a (relatively) monogamous society. They are first-generation participants in the creation of an "erotic utopia" and as such they have been imbued with many of the sexual and emotional responses programed into all of us.

"Jim,"[2] a member of an east coast urban group-marriage community, describes his situation in this way.

> The house is limping along. Jane was turned off by Ted and Ruth. . . . Ted and Ruth came in as a couple deeply turned on to each other and unprepared to share closeness with others. Also, both are pretty much down on the extended family concepts and some of the other things that Jane, Betty, Susan and I were into (Ted was really caustic at one point about encounter techniques). Basically, I think they were looking for a place to live while they pursued other things. . . . The rest of us, especially Susan, Jane and I, were looking at the house as *the* thing. I think we have all learned that neither extreme is "right," but the end result is that Ted and Ruth are moving out at the end of this month. . . . Betty and Susan are getting along beautifully. We are hosting an encounter group on a regular basis starting Friday. The kids are doing fine. The food is interesting if not always delicious . . . considering how difficult this group living is, I think we are doing well. . . . I am beginning to think that a 90 to 95 percent failure rate for group marriages and a 50 to 75 percent turn-over rate (per year) for communities might not be unrealistic. If we compare this to the situation with nuclear families (considering alienated spouses and/or children, mental illness, as well as divorces as evidence of failure) it really isn't as bad as it seems and seems to me to be much more worth the risk.[3]

Jim here cites some of the conflicts of value which are common to all communalists—loyalty to an individual versus loyalty to the group, outside interests versus group-centered interests and the like. Nonetheless, Jim's conclusion is basically optimistic. Group marriage can work. Problems associated with it can be obviated.

1. Wayne Gourley quoted in *The Modern Utopian* 2, no. 5 (May-June): p. 10.
2. The names of the communalists here have been changed.
3. Quoted in *The Modern Utopian* 4, no. 2 (Spring, 1970): 13.

From *The New Communes*

alternative to more traditional and widely accepted forms.

HOWARD'S END

by E.M. Forster
Random House, 1954

This novel is built around the lives of two English sisters, Margaret and Helen Schlegel. They are intelligent, vivacious, sensitive, "cultivated" young women of the upper-middle class, living together in London.

The lives of the Misses Schlegel intermingle with the Wilcox family. First, Helen, the younger sister, has a rather silly and brief romance with Paul Wilcox; it ends awkwardly and leaves a bad taste. Later, the Wilcoxes move to London and become neighbors of the Schlegels. Margaret Schlegel and Mrs. Wilcox become quite good friends. Mrs. Wilcox dies, having let her family know that she wants Margaret to inherit Howard's End, the family's home in the country. The Wilcoxes ignore her wish and keep the house. Eventually, the widowed Mr. Wilcox becomes involved with Margaret and marries her.

Early on, Margaret and Helen meet up with Leonard Bast, a clerk of the meagerest means trying to escape the poverty and despair of his lower-class origins. The women try to befriend him; his class-consciousness and bitterness about not belonging make that nearly impossible. Later, some casual advice given by Margaret's husband, Henry Wilcox, causes Bast to leave his apparently secure job for a lower paying one. It turns out that Wilcox's advice was ill-founded. Helen demands that Margaret insist that Henry give Bast a position; Henry refuses. His refusal causes an estrangement between the two sisters, and is the beginning of an estrangement between him and Margaret. The rift between husband and wife grows as he continues to opt for the "proper" or the profitable over the humane.

When Helen comes to her sister in great need, pregnant by Leonard Bast, Henry's selfish and wholly inappropriate response completes his estrangement with Margaret. It becomes Margaret's intention to leave him and go off with her sister. But when Henry's son Charles is convicted of the manslaughter of Bast, Henry comes to her and begs to be forgiven and cared for. From that point, she, Helen, and Henry begin to build a new, settled life together.

Helen and Margaret Schlegel are strong, independent heroines in the mold of Jane Austen's Elizabeth Bennet in *Pride and Prejudice*. Rich in plot, socially conscious, arguing human values, *Howard's End* is a novel well worth reading.

THE ODD WOMAN

by Gail Godwin
Alfred A. Knopf, Inc., 1974

It is clearly possible to study the self by studying others. We can and do learn much about who we are by observing those we care for, those we're close to, those who hold a special attraction for us. We examine their lives; we scrutinize what it is we like and dislike about them; we watch ourselves interact with them.

Jane Clifford, the protagonist of this novel, is a 30-ish single woman with a Ph.D. in literature. She teaches English at a midwestern university and moves about in a constellation of family, friends, and a lover. Jane explores herself through the people around her, growing and deepening her own sense of identity.

There is Sonia, her colleague, an outstanding professor. There is her old friend, Gerda, a universal tripper among the most current movements and causes—but not without intelligence and substance. There is her mother, Kitty, an English professor herself, rather oddly paired with a husband who cares little for the life of the mind. There is her deceased grandmother, Edith, who fills Jane's past and present with her large spirit. There is her long-dead great aunt, Cleva, a rebel who ran away with an actor. And there is her lover, Gabriel, married, showing no inclination to leave his wife for Jane. Each of these people reflects some part of Jane back to her.

The world *The Odd Woman* is set in is the intellectual world of the Academy—literature, language, ideas are very much present here, more so than pure action. In Jane

Clifford, Gail Godwin has given us a woman who demonstrates that the life of the mind needn't be coldly analytical, that intellect and the heart needn't be adversaries.

THE ODD WOMEN

by George Gissing
W.W. Norton & Company, Inc., 1971

Here's a novel written in the 1890s about several women in Victorian London. By circumstance or by choice, these women, except for one, remain single. In examining their lives, how they support each other in the daily struggle for a decent and respectable living, George Gissing demonstrates a remarkable sensitivity to the condition of women in industrial society.

Alice and Virginia Madden are left nearly penniless by their father's death. They must go to work. The work they are forced to take is grueling and so low-paying they are always on the verge of absolute destitution. They are "plain" and "beyond marriagable age," so there's no hope that they can marry out of their pulverizing circumstances. They have a younger, prettier sister, Monica, who does have the chance to get out of her miserable life as an 80-hour-a-week worker in a drapery establishment by marrying a man twice her age.

Besides the three sisters Madden there are the Misses Barfoot and Nunn, single women dedicated to training and educating other single women so they can make the best possible lives for themselves without having to settle for degrading, humiliating work. Rhoda Nunn is a tough-minded, intelligent, dedicated, pragmatic feminist. When she falls in love with her good friend's cousin, Everard Barfoot, she is forced into some agonizing decision making about her life, her work, her entire feminist point of view.

The Odd Women is a novel of Victorian England, a novel about single women helping each other, and a novel about social problems that have not yet disappeared.

Household

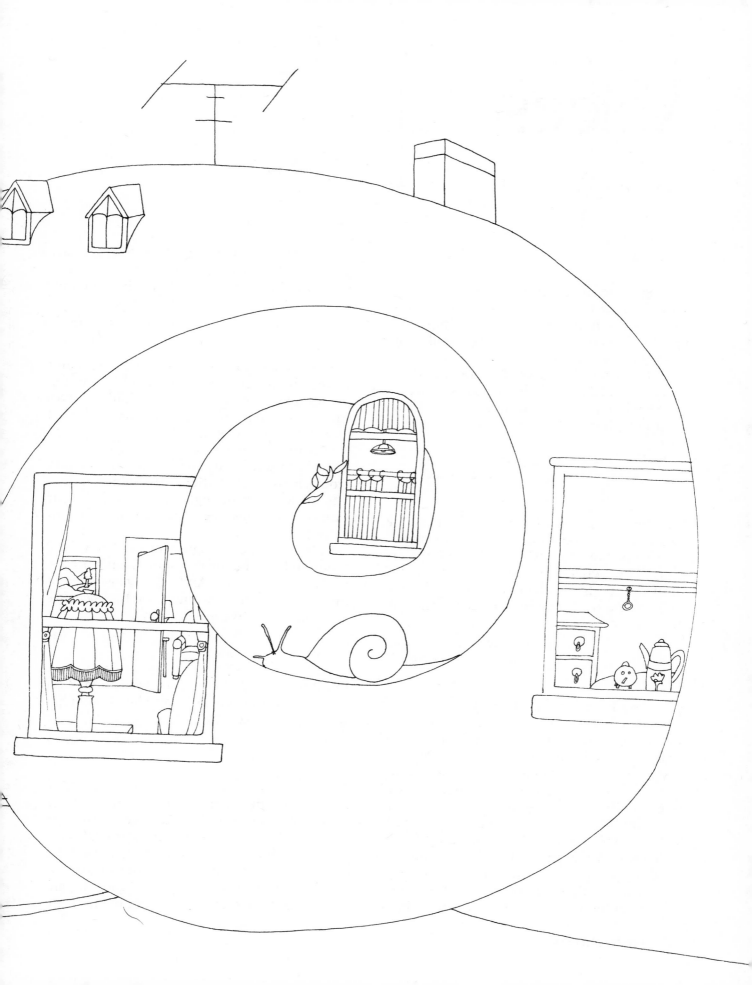

Voices

NESTING

During most of the time I was married we moved an awful lot. My older child had gone to so many schools that I felt it was important for us to put down some roots. So I said to my husband when we were splitting, "Give me half of our money because I'm going to buy a house." And I did. Over the years it's been a bit of an anchor, perhaps more of an anchor than I want now, but at the time I really felt a need for it.

Martha A., married 10 years,
divorced 5 years, age 37

Nesting is important to me. It may not look like it since I don't have a lot of furniture. That's not my style. It's not where I put my energy. But whenever I move, I put a lot of effort into finding a place that I really like to come home to. I love my house for the solitude it gives me.

Donna R., married 2 years,
divorced 7 years, age 30

After my husband died I lived a number of years in an apartment. Then I got to thinking about not wanting to be dependent on anybody. I didn't want my son and daughter-in-law to feel, "There's Grandma, what are we going to do about Grandma?" I had had the responsibility of my mother for a long time. It was very difficult for me because my father had not left her provided for. I wasn't going to let her want for anything. But I didn't want my child to have that kind of responsibility. So I looked into this retirement complex. I had two friends here already. I liked the idea that I

am completely taken care of for the rest of my life. There's a medical staff, there's maid service, and there's the communal dining room.

Eleanor M., married 32 years,
widowed 10 years, age 73

I prefer cooperative living with men and women both. I like the balance. I like sharing chores and sharing expenses. I don't like refrigerators where there's milk that's labeled "Jack's," and things like that.

It's fairly cooperative in my current apartment but there's only three of us. I like larger groups because then there's more interaction, lots of people bringing in all these different things. The house becomes a real center of activity.

I always have enough privacy. I have my room and I can shut the door. That's all the privacy I really need. And usually I get a lot of my privacy from the women that I see because generally they live alone.

Jesse F., age 34

I've often thought about getting a couch. But I feel that would be really middle class. That would be like getting a suit.

Mark B., age 28

I deliberately sought out a situation where several families shared a house. In our place there's me and my two kids, ages 6 and 7, a male single parent and his 10-year-old son, a couple with an infant, and two singles. I did not want to be isolated from other adults, living in my own apartment. Here I get companionship and my kids get companionship. They

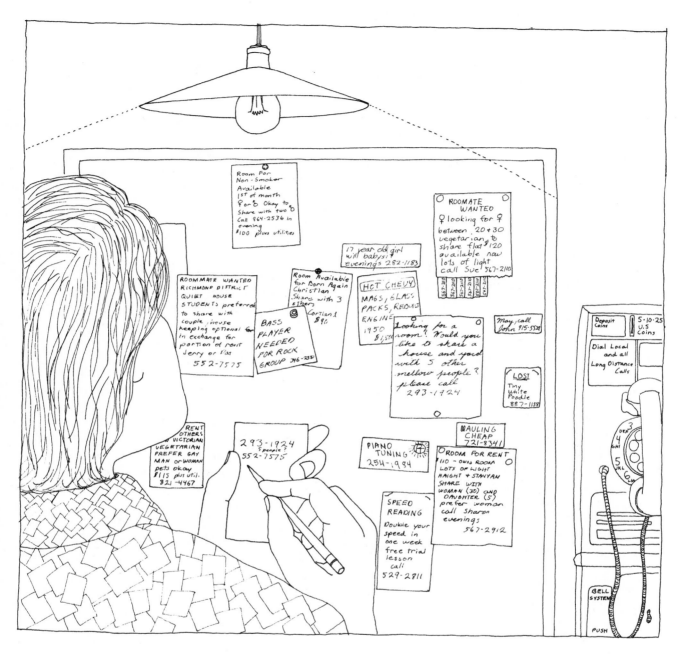

get a chance to relate to other adults, especially to men. By sharing a house this way we get to live more luxuriously than we would if we were by ourselves. Besides the huge rooms there are things like a piano and a color TV. Also, I never have to worry about getting a baby-sitter since someone is always home in the evening. There are no disadvantages that I can see because I have my own room and because I like to be around other people. This probably would be a lousy arrangement for someone who freaks out at family-style dinners or who can't stand to see other faces in the morning. But it works for me and for my kids.

Rachel B., married 10 years,
divorced 2 years, age 36

I didn't start living alone until I was about 22. Before then I had lived in a rooming house. It was a veritable looney bin, really fascinating. But after a while I began to cherish times when I was totally alone. So then I moved into an apartment, and I was suddenly very frightened. I thought, "Oh, my God, what am I doing here? I'm going to be totally alone, nobody around, nobody to talk to." But I came to love that place. And my friends came over. It got to be a place where people would meet and have dinner.

I had no furniture at first. I'd come home to this empty place. But I very quickly went out and bought what I needed. I decorated it the way I wanted to. And the most fantastic thing was that I suddenly had the total freedom of my own kitchen.

I really enjoyed decorating the place, putting things on the walls and getting a stereo. It was the first time I was able to buy things for myself. I enjoyed the idea of creating a space for myself.

Sally A., age 33

FOOD

When I'm going through some kind of turmoil I'll stop eating. The people I live with notice it. They can tell when I'm in a good space because I'll have food in the refrigerator and I'll be cooking. When I'm in a bad place they won't see me in the kitchen for five or six days. There's none of my food in the refrigerator and I come in looking like I've lost weight. So food is a good indicator of where I am.

I dislike eating out but I do when I'm on the run. When I'm eating out a lot I get frenetic. I don't like that.

When I cook for myself I make sure that I slow down. I try to make it a pure activity where I'm not mixing it in with reading or watching TV or listening to music. I just want to sit down and stop everything else and eat. I guess it's a basic animal instinct. I don't want to mix it up with something else. When I'm really in a good place I'll go out every other day to buy fresh vegetables and fish. It's a very expensive way to shop but it keeps me on top of things.

If I go for two or three weeks without food shopping, then I know I have to slow down and cook a meal and put a lot of care into my food. Another warning sign is when I get fixated on Oreo cookies. That lets me know I'm not taking good care of myself.

Larry H., married 4 years, separated 2 years, age 32

I like to eat lunch alone in restaurants. It's my pause in the day. When my co-workers ask me to join them I often turn them down, but usually I feel compelled to give an explanation. I can't just say no, which I think is terrible. I don't like to have to justify my behavior. If it's been a hectic day I need to be off by myself, just to stare out the window. But I don't like to explain that to people.

I didn't always like to eat alone in restaurants. I learned to like it on a job where I had to do a lot of traveling. That opened it up as a real possibility and sometimes a very nice experience. If my mind is full I'll just sit there in a comatose state, relaxed. I try to empty my mind. If I'm feeling O.K. otherwise and I have something I want to read, I'll do that. I usually read and eat at home, so I'm used to it.

At home I eat quick dinners. A lot of times I don't want to bother. It's not junk but then again it isn't a whole meal. I never eat leftovers. I don't believe in them. The spoiled child syndrome. I throw them away, even though I know people are starving in India.

I don't really plan my meals, I eat whatever is there. It's easy for me to get into a rut. I get out of it when that particular food runs out. Then I don't buy that thing again for a while.

Donna R., married 2 years, divorced 7 years, age 30

I'm proud of the fact that I have not eaten out at a restaurant for the past seven months. I feel I can prepare a more economical, better-balanced meal at home. I'm not fancy, but I can prepare a decent meal. And I receive a certain sense of satisfaction from it. I enjoy the manual aspects of preparing it. All day I'm caught up in the academic world and the realm of the mind. I like to get home and cut up a piece of beef or set the table. No matter how simple it is, just watching some type of food take edible shape gives me pleasure. I usually have music going. I feel good about it. I'm never too tired or too rushed to cook dinner. I look forward to that hour of preparing and eating the meal. I always do it before I begin my evening's activities.

I create a pretty enjoyable atmosphere for eating. I keep items of interest on the table— some favorite shells, a couple of books, some poems, whatever.

Occasionally I get so hungry because I've skipped lunch that I find myself bent over the plate, kind of shoveling the food into my mouth, just losing control of the proper pace for eating. I'll tell myself, "My God, you're eating like a Neanderthal. Slow down. You can preserve some of the social graces although you're eating alone."

George P., age 25

We have a communal dining room here and the food is excellent. But I often skip it and eat soup or cheese in my room. I like to read and I don't enjoy sitting at the table listening to all the gossip. I'm not trying to make myself out as an intellectual, but I have other things I can do than sit and listen to such little talk.

When I eat in the dining room, however, I'll sit with a group. I don't want people to think I want to be alone.

Eleanor M., married 32 years, widowed 10 years, age 73

I eat alone a lot. I like to eat alone. I always have good food, and I eat in the kitchen on my stool. I never watch television while I eat. I just eat. I read a book by Fritz Perls, who said, "Whatever you do, do it and enjoy it." That's what I do—I eat and enjoy what I'm eating. It's a pleasure to be here in my house. I cook such good food and it's so quiet. I'd rather be here than in a restaurant.

Ellen B., married 22 years, divorced 3 years, age 58

I don't go in for elaborate meals. I like to throw things into a pan and add spices. I enjoy soups and chili and hash. Never anything elegant.

I resist food fixations. I have a friend who gets on a thing, who eats the same dinner for weeks. Then he'll change over to something new and then eat that for maybe a month. I don't do that. A general part of my personality is that I hate to do the same thing twice.

I try to shop as little as possible. I keep a lot of canned goods and freezer items on hand. I don't have leftovers because I either eat everything I prepare or share it with someone else who happens to come into the kitchen.

Max F., age 29

I don't eat very well when I eat alone. Whenever I live alone the food ceases to be an event. When I'm in a family or group situation I really care about food a lot. It becomes a kind of gift that I prepare as a way of showing love.

I don't like to eat alone in restaurants. I always feel that people are watching me, and they're sort of singling me out and saying, "Look at that poor person. He's eating alone. That's really pathetic." I'm very other-directed about that.

Jesse F., age 34

I eat dinner in front of the television set. It's a bit more companionable than sitting in the kitchen alone, and I don't happen to read while I'm eating dinner. I read the paper while I'm eating breakfast, but I have just gotten into the habit of mixing the news with dinner.

Lynn H., age 45

I eat out in restaurants a lot. It's partly because I travel so much, but also I just don't enjoy cooking for myself. That leads me to eat a lot of junk food. I play a lot of sports after work and I don't have enough strength to go and cook a meal. So I just go out and get a hamburger. I've probably never used the oven in my apartment. In fact, I don't know how to use the oven.

Wherever I eat, it's usually alone. I almost always read while I eat, even in fancy restaurants.

I'm concerned about having a balanced diet. Since mine isn't, I take a lot of vitamins. I feel like the vitamins are going to balance off the crap.

Patrick R., married 4 years, divorced 2 years, age 34

Dinner is always a full meal. Nights when I am rushed, I'll grab something in a Chinese restaurant. But it's still a whole dinner. I prefer making dinner for myself. I like setting out a nice plate and having a salad. Food is very sensuous. It's also a thing to bring people together. I'll just call a friend and say, "Hi, I just made a pot roast. Make a salad, I'm coming over."

Sally A., age 33

UPKEEP

Repairs are a big problem. I really like mechanical men and engineers because they can help me a great deal. I can't take care of this house by myself. My ex-husband is in the construction business so I have a lot of helpful friends. I do play male-female games in getting men to help me fix my house. I always say that I feel I've been exploited by men and not treated enough like a person. But I admit I play the other side of it too.

*Jennifer F., married 5 years,
divorced 5 years, age 34*

The thing about housekeeping is that it's a great pleasure. I love to run around the house and keep it clean.

*Ellen B., married 22 years,
divorced 3 years, age 58*

I don't have many dishes to wash. Usually I don't even eat off dishes. I eat out of the pan.
And I wouldn't dare do repairs. I'm about the least handy person in the world. I'll call the landlord when there's a problem.

*Patrick R., married 4 years,
divorced 2 years, age 34*

My feminist solution to working five days a week and keeping my house the way I like it is to have cleaning men. They come while I'm at work, bring all their own equipment, and do all the heavy, time-consuming maintenance that I hate: waxing floors, emptying the fireplace of ashes, cleaning the oven, scouring the tub.

Sara C., age 31

I hardly ever do it. I let the dishes pile up. It's really nice not having someone around to gripe about them.

Cindy W., age 24

I use housekeeping as a way of knowing where I am. Like if I'm rushing too fast and I'm not paying attention to my own needs, my room is sloppy. There are books all over the place, there are papers all over, my bed's not made, there's dust, the floor needs vacuuming.

*Larry H., married 4 years,
separated 2 years, age 32*

I spend very little time housecleaning now because I have nobody to stand back and criticize me.

*Adele F., married 30 years,
widowed 1 year, age 59*

Dining Alone

M.F.K. FISHER

Lucullus, the Roman host whose dinners are still talked about for their elaborate menus and their fabulous cost, grew tired one day of dining with other men.

He ordered a meal for one person. When it was served to him, he was conscious of a certain slackness: the wine was perhaps a shade too cold, and the sauce for the carp, which certainly was less succulent than usual, lacked that tang for which his chef was justly famed.

Lucullus frowned and summoned the major-domo.

"Perhaps, perhaps," that official agreed, with a flood of respectful salutations. "We thought that there was no need to prepare a fine banquet for my lord alone . . ."

"It is precisely when I am alone," the great gourmet answered, icily, "that you require to pay special attention to the dinner. At such times, you must remember, Lucullus dines with Lucullus."

At such times few men realize that they are dining with themselves. In fact, they try to forget that rather frightening truth. They read the newspaper or turn on the radio if they are at home. More often they flee from themselves to friend-filled clubs, or to the noisiest nearest restaurant, where other lone humans eat crowded together in a hungry, ugly mob and take digestive pills between their hurried courses.

It is a pity. An occasional meal with himself is very good for Mr. Doe. It gives him time to look about him; quiet in which to savour his present mouthful; opportunity to broil his steak a new way or try again those dishes his wife hates.

He need not take it too seriously, however. Old Thomas Walker, The Original, whose preoccupation with the fine points of dining approached pomposity at times, declared himself thus on the problem:

"When dining alone is necessary, the mind should be disposed to cheerfulness by a previous interval of relaxation from whatever has seriously occupied the attention, and be directing it to some agreeable object."

The "interval of relaxation" might well be used for broiling a tender filet although I doubt if Mr. Walker meant just that; and there could be no more "agreeable object" toward which to direct attention than a fine little bottle of red wine from the Côte d'Or. There with a leaf or two of salad and some crusty sour-dough bread, Lucullus has a meal fit even for Lucullus.

An Englishman, however, and an earl at that, once mapped out a slightly more complicated menu.

"A good soup," he said, "a small turbot, a neck of venison, ducklings with green peas or chicken with asparagus, and an apricot tart—it is a dinner for an emperor."

Perhaps he was right. Louis XIV of France, who always dined alone at one o'clock, ate several soups, three solid courses, and then a dessert.

He also ate only from a square table, and was served by nobles of his court, both facts probably influencing his digestion to a certain extent. (Many people enjoy good food only to the sound of soft music, or in a room with black walls. My mother cannot swallow if a cat is near her. Hunger, I observe, is not a part of these equations.)

I have known two people who understood, and probably without one thought about it, why Lucullus dined with Lucullus. One was

Many people enjoy good food only to the sound of soft music, or in a room with black walls.

an old man, the other a girl sixteen and usually inarticulate.

Biddy was tall and quiet, with magnificent brown eyes and the stiff awkwardness of a new-hatched butterfly. She lived in a kind of daze, seemingly placid, lethargic, docilely stubborn.

One day she took her week's allowance and moved tranquilly and relentlessly towards the tram, muttering of errands and birthdays and such. To her mother's puzzled questions she smiled reassurance, vague but firm.

Late that afternoon she came back.

She brought no birthday presents nor evidences of errands done, but one rather spotted paper bag, from which she drew a long brown cut of *apfelstrudel* for her mother. She was vaguer than usual, but seemed to be unharmed—and the *strudel* was delicious.

Later I saw Biddy. We were talking of restaurants. I saw her eyes flash suddenly when I mentioned Spring Street in Los Angeles, where, one man said, the best and worst food in seven states can be found in less than as many blocks.

"I hear you went to town last Saturday," I said, feeling like Sherlock Holmes and Tom the Peeper. "What did you do?"

Biddy looked quickly at me, and then smiled rather sheepishly.

"Spring Street, eh? Where did you go?"

"Well—I went to *Katie Levey's*. And why haven't you told me how good it is? And the people!"

"Lots of Austrian Jews, I suppose?"

"Naturally, in a kosher restaurant run by a Viennese! Of course," she added carelessly, "Jews are the best indication of good food in a place."

I nodded recognition to one of her mother's favourite remarks, and asked, "But what did you do from eleven to three? You can't eat lunch for four hours."

Biddy answered me somewhat scornfully: "I ate breakfast, not lunch, and certainly I ate it for four hours: they understand things like that in a decent restaurant. I drank coffee, with lots of hot milk in it, and ate Viennese tarts and—and things."

"Things meaning salami and sweet pickles?"

"Mhm."

She looked dreamily past me. I said nothing, and finally she went on: "I sat by the cake counter and watched people in the mirror. They were so queer—so *pleasant* at eleven when everybody else in town was rushing around—and especially down there on Spring. And they spoke every language and dipped their tarts in their coffee-glasses.

"Yes," Biddy exclaimed, "my coffee was in a glass! It was wonderful!"

Her face was vivid, and in her dark eyes was a quiet awareness I had never seen before. She concluded, almost fiercely: "Four hours I sat there, watching them dip their bread in coffee-glasses, and thinking. And I'll do it again! It was—it was just what I needed."

Biddy breakfasted with Biddy, and saw in a mirror clearly, for the first of many times.

From *The Art of Eating* by M.F.K. Fisher

Books

COOKING FOR ONE IS FUN

by Henry Lewis Creel
Quadrangle, 1976

For some singles, cooking is a rather grim and relentless necessity. For others, it's comme ci, comme ça. And for still others, cooking a meal is one of life's chief delights. For this last group, along comes *Cooking for One is Fun*. The recipes here are not simply make-the-best-of-a-middling-situation-by-adding-a-can-of-cream-of-mushroom-soup. Rather, they are recipes for those with real commitment to fine cooking and fine eating.

The author washed dishes for years for Craig Claiborne and Pierre Franey, and obviously learned much from those two masters. His recipes, each for one person, pay particular attention to those simple yet exquisite touches that can change an O.K. dish into a splendid one—a T of cognac in the ground beef, dry mustard and vermouth with the pork chops.

Many of the recipes have those delightful and unexpected fillips, resulting in interesting and delicious combinations of flavors that help make eating more than a simple act of refueling.

COOKING FOR ONE

by Elinor Parker
Thomas Y. Crowell Co., 1976

Cooking for One has more than 250 recipes tailored for one-person meals. For the most part the recipes produce relatively quick, sensible, straightforward dinners—nothing really fancy or grand. Still, it will greatly expand the repertoire of any single cook whose meal preparation runs the gamut from meat and potatoes to potatoes and meat.

Parker covers all the necessaries amply—soup, salad, meat, vegetables, cheese, rice, macaroni, eggs, dessert. Beyond that she has some wonderfully useful sections on kitchen equipment (including a complete inventory of supplies and another list of staples for your cupboard), helpful hints, uses for leftover ingredients, prepared products. She includes a good chapter on menus and another one on entertaining singlehandedly.

All in all, *Cooking for One* is a practical book for the single cook who doesn't fancy her- or himself the chef d' hôtel, but is ready to try something more daring than grilled cheese.

APPENDIX TO THE I HATE TO COOK BOOK

by Peg Bracken
Fawcett Publications, 1966

Peg Bracken has probably lightened the loads of millions of American women by wisecracking her way through the hallowed halls of housewifery. But she's not only a gagster, she's a collector of marvelously useful tidbits of information that help to ease the lives of those who don't much like housework and cooking.

And who says it's only housewives who hate all the fuss and bother of preparing meals? Could very well be there are just as many single folks, male and female, who feel exactly the same way. And often they don't even have the incentive of preparing a meal for the rave reviews the family cook might be rewarded with.

The *Appendix to the I Hate to Cook Book* is a good book for singles who want to spend as little time in the kitchen as possible, and who

ALONE, COOKING IF

The problem hasn't really been solved by several recent books on the subject, which tell you how to make Pickled-Beet-and-Macaroni Salad for One, or Ox Tongue with Raisin for One, and that sort of thing.

These books don't get to the heart of it. Their authors, who obviously like to cook, have no idea what people who don't are willing to put up with, in exchange for the sheer joy of not cooking.

While there are recipes in this chapter, they are recipes of a different kind. The truth is, anyone who has trouble getting the lead out of her lingerie to cook for other people will find it all but impossible to do so for herself. The minimal cooking done in these situations is truly breath-taking.

I know an elderly lady whose breakfast is whole-wheat toast, bacon, and coffee; whose lunch is a vitamin pill with a Met-recal chaser; and whose dinner is an Old-Fashioned and something frozen, whatever she bumps into first in her fair-sized frozen-food compartment. She's the healthiest elderly lady you ever saw, too, as I happen to know, because she is my mother.

I also know a man who lives alone—hates to cook—and never tires of frozen spinach soufflé, which is fortunate, because that's all he ever has for dinner at home besides a pan-broiled chop or a steak. Sometimes he pours canned cheese sauce on the soufflé. Not always.

And I know a girl who leans heavily on eggs. Hard-boiled. Soft-boiled. Scrambled. Or, in rare moments of culinary enterprise, in a Spanish omelet. She simmers, in butter, some onion, green pepper, and chopped fresh tomato (I believe that's where the Spanish comes in). Then she pours it over the omelet.

I asked her if she didn't get tired of eggs, and she cackled that she did, but they were still better than cooking.

—But enough of case histories, and back to the Prime Rib.

BACHELOR'S BEEF, OR HOW TO COOK A PRIME RIB FOR ONE

Ask the butcher for 1 rib of a standing rib roast. This will weigh around two and a half pounds.

It's important that you freeze it, because it must be roasted frozen. So wrap it in freezer foil and do so. (You should have thought of this yesterday.)

Next day or next month, an hour and a half before you want to eat, take it out, unwrap it, and rub it all over with garlic, if you like garlic, and then a tablespoon of salad oil or olive oil.

Stand it on its side in a baking pan, propped against two scrubbed or peeled baking potatoes.

Roast it at 400° for one hour and twenty-five minutes if you like it rare; ten minutes more if you like it fairly well done. Let it stand five minutes before you slice it.

I did this one night when I had a guest. There was enough left over for good cold beef the next night and several sandwiches thereafter, which I consider a good bargain.

From Appendix to the I Hate to Cook Book

don't much care about gourmet dinners. The first chapter, as a matter of fact, is just for singles. Bracken writes:

"It is a barefooted fact that cooking and eating alone can be remarkably relaxing. There is no one to comment on the fact that it's meatloaf again and no dessert, or to interrupt with larger issues when you want to talk about smaller ones, and vice versa. Not that it is completely clear sailing, even so. One of the reefs that can hang you up, when you hate to cook, is that some of the best things are big. For instance, an important thing to know about cooking for yourself is how to cook a Prime Rib for one person."

Bracken tells how, gives 140 other recipes, and at least twice that many jokes.

MICROWAVE COOK BOOK

by the editors of Sunset Books and
Sunset Magazine
Lane Publishing Company, 1976

The microwave oven is a dream come true for those who can't or don't want to spend large bunches of their time in the kitchen. Cook pork chops in five minutes. Bake a potato in four minutes. A lemon meringue pie in three minutes. Lobster tails in two minutes. Appetizers in a minute.

This book provides a good primer on the workings of the microwave oven and the hows and wherefores of this speedy kind of cooking. The recipes are varied and imaginative—everything from Athenia Moussaka to Lasagne Belmonte to Zucchini and Rice Pilaf. The book, however, isn't written for singles, so you can either use the recipes for entertaining or do some of that old familiar singles math and divide everything by four, six, or eight.

THE I HATE TO HOUSEKEEP BOOK

by Peg Bracken
Fawcett Publications, 1962

Written back in the 1950s, this book addresses itself to housewives and calls them "girls" and "gals." If you can overlook that,

you'll find it to be a valuable little manual that provides a passel and a half of hints for making housework quite a bit swifter and easier.

Bracken's strategy of housekeeping is to sustain a "modest modicum of order" that leaves time for other things besides chasing dust and emptying ashtrays. To carry out that strategy she equips the housekeeper with weapons against everything from stains to scratched furniture to blown fuses. Her tips are always useful and very often original: "A good thing to do with your freezer is to keep your sneakers in it, on hot summer days. Wash the pair you're not wearing in the washer, dry them in the dryer, then freeze them in cellophane bags. When you put on your freshly-frozen sneakers, they'll keep your feet cool for a couple of hours, even in very hot weather."

If you're a spotless housekeeper you won't need this book. But if you're like those of us whose chief aim is simply to keep from getting engulfed in a tidal wave of clutter, you'll likely find some help in *The I Hate to Housekeep Book*.

TAKE CARE OF YOURSELF: A CONSUMER'S GUIDE TO MEDICAL CARE

by Donald M. Vickery and James F. Fries
Addison-Wesley, 1976

"For the most part, " write the physician authors of *Take Care of Yourself*, "you can do more for your health than your doctor can." And the bill for your services won't add to your pains.

Doctors Vickery and Fries have been involved in training para-medical professionals and in computerized medicine. They have tapped these experiences in a kind of paper computer that helps you decide what you can do to treat yourself and when you should seek professional help.

The guts of the book are 68 two-page spreads on troubles ranging from cuts and burns to dandruff to chest pains to hemorrhoids. Each spread discusses the given ailment in easy-to-understand terms, outlines a home treatment program, and previews what to expect if you take your complaint to the doctor. A simple flow-chart with direct questions helps you decide whether to apply the home treatment or seek professional help.

The book is hardly anti-physician. The authors make it clear that when in doubt, don't treat yourself. But they want lay people to know that in many, many cases, doctors can't do much for you except charge you for an office visit and give you the same kind of advice that you'll find here.

The book is wonderfully organized; when a problem arises, you'll have no trouble finding out what to do about it. But even when you're feeling fine, you might enjoy browsing through the catalogue of misfortunes that at the moment aren't befalling you. At the same time, you'll find the reading an interesting antidote to the medical nonsense beamed your way on the tube.

LIVING IN ONE ROOM

by Jon Naar and Molly Siple
Vintage Books, 1976

In all those old Russian short stories the consumptive little clerk finished his scrivening late at night, put on his tattered overcoat, walked miles through the snow to his tiny, barren room, heated up his samovar and wrote a few paragraphs of his novel until his fingers were stiff with the cold. Now if the room he came home to was like any of those in this book, he'd surely have been encouraged to quit his job, finish his novel, trade his samovar for an espresso machine, and become the toast of all Moscow. That's the kind of room Naar and Siple present in *Living in One Room*: imaginative, vivacious, appealing rooms. Whatever their actual size, most *feel* roomy.

Making a single room into a rich living space requires a kind of artistic boldness, imagination, and skill that many of us simply don't have in ample quantities. The real value of this book is its supply of that boldness, imagination, and skill. Here is nearly every sort of single-room apartment and a cornucopia of strategies for designing within limited spaces. The authors cover a variety of subjects: sleeping, cooking, entertaining, working, storage, and others. The book is primarily visual, aiming to stimulate your creative juices with photographs. One might wish for more text, giving lots of practical details. But that is a small cavil, since it is clear the chief purpose of the book is to help us see that a single-room apartment can be a rich, roomy, and functional living space.

THE READER'S DIGEST COMPLETE DO-IT-YOURSELF MANUAL

W.W. Norton & Company, Inc., 1973

Many of us, when writing those large checks to the plumber, the electrician, the carpenter, have the sneaking suspicion that those repairs weren't so complicated after all, that we might have been able to make them ourselves if we weren't such schlemiels. Yet to anyone who numbers her- or himself among the many-thumbed, the merest thought of doing any home-repair job causes heart flutters and hyperventilation.

The fact is there are a remarkable number of home repairs even the clumsiest of us can execute, if not deftly at least respectably; and in so doing, save a bundle in repairperson's fees. *The Reader's Digest Complete Do-It-Yourself Manual* is an excellent guide for the home handyperson. Its 17 sections cover everything from plumbing to electricity to brickwork to woodwork to painting to glass, ceramics, and plastics. The text is clear and the illustrations are, generally, excellent— simple, uncluttered, easy to understand.

Loving

Voices

FINDING SOMEONE

The incredible number of divorces has really changed things, because many of the divorced women are stuck out in tract houses with the kids. Most of the divorced guys, on the other hand, are free agents. And what that does to someone like me is it cuts down on the odds. Because now you've got this whole batch of reborn single males to compete with.

Tom E., age 30

I will never say no when a friend says, "Hey, I'd like you to meet someone." I want to be totally open and available for any type of new meeting and encounter. Even if I'm tired, not feeling too well, doubtful, dubious, whatever, I'll usually make the effort to meet someone and consider the possibility, "This could be someone important. This could be someone wonderful."

George P., age 25

I don't date for the simple reason that there's nobody around for me to date. I can't be interested in anybody younger than I am. Young people have so many complications. They're so screwed up. I don't want to cope with that. I've been through it all in my life already.

As for men my age, I don't see them. Where in the hell are they? They're not piling up on my doorstep, that's for sure. I think the men my age are all with the younger women. I went to a lecture and there were two men about my age and I thought, "Mmmmmm." But it turned out they're both living with 30-year-old girls.

Actually, I'm not that interested in finding a man. For a while I was until I realized I wanted someone just to add a little excitement to my life. Then I decided I ought to make my own excitement. I can't depend on someone else.

Ellen B., married 22 years,
divorced 3 years, age 58

I go out occasionally, to the symphony or to parties. But men my age are interested in ladies much younger than I am. Let's face it. Yes, that's the way it is. I don't understand it. In fact, it should be to the contrary. Women should go out with younger men because I can run circles around most of the men my age.

Eleanor M., married 32 years,
widowed 10 years, age 73

It seems very strange to me that there should be so many individuals who want to be married or have a love relationship and yet it is so hard for one individual to find another. There ought to be the old-fashioned big affairs where you had these hoards of men and these hoards of women playing some game like "Find the Shoe," where all the women's shoes are thrown in the middle of the floor and you date the person whose shoe you get.

Max F., age 29

I live in a big singles neighborhood. All the single women around here, in their 30s or so, are very involved in fixing up their

women or men friends with other people. I've never lived in this kind of singles network before. It's really something. There's an unwritten law that you never go out with a man—or fix him up with a friend—during the first year he's separated from his partner. He's what's called an "untouchable." Untouchables are people fresh from a split-up who are very wrapped up in their traumas, who can't reach out, who are very bewildered and confused, who can't give a lot of caring, who just really need a lot. And women who get mixed up with these men find that it doesn't usually work out. So that's why they call them the untouchables. A woman I recently started going with told me that I was an untouchable because I split up from my partner only four months ago. But she says she doesn't care.

I can sort of understand the untouchable thing, though. I slept with a woman not long ago and told her I would spend the night with her. But I woke up around one in the morning and just couldn't stay with her. I

got up and tried to see my former girl friend. So I am really going through a crazy period. I don't know how long it will take.

Jesse F., age 34

If I'm attracted to a man, I run around and ask people we know in common to tell me about him. If I decide I want to get to know him better, I will pursue him. I'll have a dinner party and invite him over or figure out a way to see him. I try to put myself in the situation where I am completely in control of how fast it progresses. I don't want to be an available piece of meat in the local singles market.

I like to do just about anything on a date. I'm most flattered if a man invites me to his friends' house for dinner. That's nice because he's introducing me to his friends. I also appreciate it if he finds a baby-sitter when I can't come up with one.

I usually offer to split the cost of things like movies or dinners. Half the men accept.

I don't have strong feelings about it. But the men who want to pay the whole thing know that I won't pay them back sexually. It's so out in the open now that if I offer to pay and they don't want me to, they'll say, "Don't worry. You don't have to sleep with me."

Jennifer F., married 5 years,
divorced 5 years, age 34

I like to juggle a lot of relationships at one time. One woman I was going with from another town said to me, "Larry, I hate to think of what you're doing when I'm not around. All I imagine is that there's a lady hiding behind every bush. Is there anybody else?"

And I said, "Don't ask me that because you're not going to like the answer."

And she said, "Well, how many are there?"

And I said, "Thirteen." She was very mad at that answer.

Of course, the number fluctuates. Sometimes what happens is somebody will say, "I'm not sleeping with you any more. And the reason is because I don't want the relationship to stop when we stop going to bed together. So I just want to see you outside the bedroom." That can work out when there's a heavy foundation of friendship.

Larry H., married 4 years,
separated 2 years, age 32

I'm not interested in being fixed up. I guess people figure that if you're alone you must be lonely. It's as if your life needed to be fixed up. But that's not the case. I was really relieved when people stopped trying to fix me up. Then I could relax and just enjoy myself.

Holly H., married 3 years,
divorced 3 years, age 29

I meet women mostly through friends, though sometimes just walking down the street. I'll say "hello" and just start talking. In the City, a lot of women are afraid of that,

afraid of strangers. But at the same time, I find women are a bit more aggressive than they were before I got married. They seem to have read a lot of manuals about how things should be. But I kind of like that. I like the fact that women should be equals in all ways. I don't have any problems with that. I don't feel threatened. I feel that's a very healthy way to be.

Patrick R., married 4 years,
divorced 2 years, age 34

LOVE AND SEX

When I don't have somebody I'm sleeping with I just don't think about it, even though I feel that I'm a very sensual and sexual person. I rarely get horny. But one thing I do miss is being held by someone. I can fill that need, though, by telling a friend, "I need a hug right now." Everybody's willing to oblige.

I'd much rather do that than have casual affairs. I went through that when I was younger and it isn't worth it to me. I don't like waking up to somebody that I don't know. I want to be able to say, "Hello, you want breakfast?" and not feel I'm talking to a stranger.

If I do need something sexually but there's no one around that I care about, I would rather have me and my left hand than a man I don't know.

Sally A., age 33

The act itself really means less to me than just being with the person. I look more for the emotional contact than the sexual contact.

Bruce F., married 10 years,
separated 2 years, age 38

Sex has no importance at all right now. I had a very good sexual relationship with my husband. I miss it but not like I thought I would. It seems like when he left, it took that thing out of my life, which was really nice. Then I had this boy friend and he was a terrible lover. After I finally taught him how to make love to me, he found a 32-year-old girl. So that was the end of that. I think my subconscious took over and decided I wasn't going to mess myself up with that kind of desire any more. A little bit of longing, occasionally, but not much.

Ellen B., married 22 years,
divorced 3 years, age 58

I'm not too good at casual sexual relationships any more. I was good at them at one time. I think I've got that out of my system.

Patrick R., married 4 years,
divorced 2 years, age 34

I had a few dates in the first two years after my divorce. Then there were two years of celibacy, which I didn't like at all. Finally, a younger friend encouraged me to go out. I went to bars a few times with her and I met a couple of men at parties and bam, everything started. "Post-divorce sexual frenzy" somebody called it. I think that's the right term. I was really forcing myself to do it. I learned a lot and got a lot of experience but also felt guilt and anxiety.

One thing I am encountering is the phenomenon of men who are not really anxious to go to bed. Women sort of grow up with the idea that all men are always eager for sex. But I'm more ready than they are and that's kind of disconcerting because I tend to think, "Well, who wouldn't want to go to bed with me?" They seem to feel that it's premature or that they want to get to know me better first, or something like that. You expect a woman to react that way, not a man.

I've had just one one-nighter. It was very ungratifying, especially since I caught V.D. from it.

Martha A., married 10 years,
divorced 5 years, age 37

SEX ALONE

Masturbation is quite important, but I don't make a big deal out of it. I did read in Hemingway's *A Farewell to Arms* about men who would buy a certain type of very soft, ripe melon and masturbate into it. That's quite removed from my own experience. I do it quickly and get it over with rather than think about where I can find ripe Spanish melons. But I like the idea of making it more special. That seems to go along with finding happiness by oneself.

George P., age 25

I want to be with a man . . . until I start to masturbate. But when I get into my fantasy and after I've had an orgasm, then it doesn't bug me that I didn't have it with a man.

Cindy W., age 24

It's—how do I find the word?—*necessary.* I do it every day. It's like exercising. There are pressures that build up and I think too much attention is attracted to the sexual area if you don't release those tensions.

It can lessen the need to have sex with a woman. I'll masturbate sometimes before going out. I don't want to be driven by my gonads. I want it to be first and foremost a relationship between people, then, secondarily, a sexual relationship.

Max F., age 29

I don't mind being celibate. I never masturbate. When there's nobody I really like, I'm not interested. I've never had a sex drive that wasn't focused on one particular person. I never thought about masturbation until the women's movement started talking about it and you were supposed to do it. It sounded great. I was open to it and tried it. But nothing happened. I got bored and gave up. That's the story of that.

Jennifer F., married 5 years,
divorced 5 years, age 34

SEX WITH MARRIEDS

There was a time when I felt very strongly that I would not have sex with a married man. Now I feel that it's possible in the situation where the wife knew. I think it would be important for me to feel that this was not something behind someone else's back. It would have to be some mutual arrangement.

*Donna R., married 2 years,
divorced 7 years, age 30*

Love it. That doesn't make any difference. As long as no one knows about it.

Jesse F., age 34

I've never done it. It would bother me. I'm not exactly sure why. I guess I feel it's sneaky. I wouldn't feel comfortable doing it.

*Patrick R., married 4 years,
divorced 2 years, age 34*

Many of my married women friends ask me to invite their husbands over while they're away. The wives have infinite trust in their husbands. I know better. Lots of married men have gone after me. But I never tell their wives. I keep the peace very nicely by not getting involved. I just say politely to the man, "I identify with your wife." That usually does it.

*Jennifer F., married 5 years,
divorced 5 years, age 34*

I'm always afraid of getting my head shot off so I tend to stay away from that.

Tom E., age 30

I have had sex with married men who I have known for a long time and really care about. I don't believe in couple relationships.

Ruth G., age 46

An old boy friend showed up one day. He was on a business trip. He said he wanted to marry me but he didn't want to give up his wife. He wanted to be a bigamist. He had made a very definite decision about that. He said he could not live without me and yet he loved his wife. I said, "If you tell your wife about this, then it's fine. If she agrees to it, O.K." And, of course, he would never have done that.

Sally A., age 33

You and Others

PHILIP ZIMBARDO

How much do you know about your own personal brand of shyness? Or how well are you tuned in to the shyness of those you live with and work with? What turns on those feelings of shyness? How often do they occur? How strong are they? What are you feeling and thinking when shyness comes your way? Which behaviors are telltale outward signs of what you are experiencing inside? What have you done to handle such reactions in the past?

By reflecting upon the causes, correlates and consequences of your shyness, you gain two important benefits. First, you are laying the groundwork for a rational plan of intervention, treatment or change. In addition, by explicitly analyzing the nature and dimensions of personal shyness, you begin to turn it out, to distance yourself from it by objectifying it. This allows you to get a better perspective on that inner distress you want to avoid or run away from. In a sense, I'd like you to put your shyness on a psychological operating table and approach it with the cool "detached concern" of a surgeon carefully inspecting it before deciding where and how to proceed with the operation.

How did your shyness develop?

Write a letter talking about how your shyness developed. In your letter, cover the following points:

- What is the *first* time that you remember feeling shy? Describe the situation, people involved, and your feelings.
  a) What decisions about yourself did you make based on this experience?
  b) Did others say anything to you that made you think that you were shy? What exactly did they say? What decisions did you make at that time about yourself based on what they said?
  c) Can you now see that there was a misinterpretation involved (of motives, responsibility, or missed signals)? Describe what really took place and how it was distorted.
  d) Did anyone do anything to make you feel better (less shy), or worse? Who?
  e) Have those decisions you've made about yourself changed over the years or have they remained about the same?
- What is the *next* time that you remember feeling shy?
- Think about another time during your childhood, then during your teen years, and then this last year when you've felt most shy. Do the same things still make you feel shy?
- Do people say things to you now that lead you to think of yourself as shy? What?
- Do you let other people know that you are a shy person? How do you signal this, and how soon after meeting someone do you communicate this message?
  Do you ever do or say things that make other people in your life feel shy?

Costs and benefits

What has being shy cost you? What opportunities have you passed up and experiences forfeited because you are or were shy? Make an itemized cost accounting of each thing you have lost, given up, or settled for less of.

Now think very hard about the subtle things you have gained from pasting that shyness label on yourself. Most of us learn how to

You can let your ideal person know you are ready and willing, although you have no idea what his/her response will be.

derive something positive even from adversity. What do you get out of your shyness? Since we don't usually acknowledge these "secondary gains" of our primary disabilities, some examples may be in order: excuses, playing it safe and not taking unnecessary risks, avoiding criticism, keeping aggressive people away, not becoming emotional or too involved in other people's lives, etc. Make an itemized accounting of these gains.

Rejection

Write down some past rejections that hurt you a great deal. Then, write down the areas in which you are most sensitive to rejection. What is the worst thing that can happen in each of these areas (how could the rejection have been even worse)? In what areas can you tolerate rejection, shrug off put-downs? Is there any basic difference between these two general areas of vulnerability and invulnerability?

Try to imagine scenarios in which some of these unpleasant rejections turned out to be not as bad after all—that is, the rejection was not intended as such, was misperceived by you, was funny, or taught you a valuable lesson. Write brief scripts to accompany these scenarios for several rejection episodes.

Taking risks

You can try for the $100,000 prize—winner takes all, loser gets nothing—or you can pass it up and be certain of winning $5,000. Do you take the risk or settle for the sure thing?

You can go on a date with a so-so person who you know will definitely accept, or you can let your ideal person know you are ready and willing, although you have no idea what his/her response will be. Do you stand pat with your two pairs or gamble on a full house?

List all the important chances, risks, and gambles that you have taken in your life. Next to each, note whether it proved wise or foolish.

Now go out and take a risk. Do something "scary" that you would like to, ought to, but have been avoiding. Do one scary thing every day this week, first writing down what you intend to do and why it is scary for you. Then record whether or not you did it, and what happened when you did. Of course, I mean socially scary, not scary like robbing a bank or jumping from the Golden Gate Bridge.

From *Shyness* by Philip Zimbardo

Books

THE HITE REPORT

by Shere Hite
Dell Books, 1976

Shere Hite can claim a place in the pantheon of sex researchers not particularly because of her scientific expertise or the rigor of her methods, but because she had the uncommonly good sense to ask thousands of women to say exactly how they experience sex and what they think about it, and then publish the results for us all to share. *The Hite Report* is a necessary and important book because it compiles the understanding of the real experts, telling about what they know best—their own experiences.

Hite received 3000 replies to the 100,000 questionnaires she sent out. She was fortunate to hear from women who were articulate and direct, for it is their answers which give this book its substance. They answered detailed questions about masturbation, orgasm, intercourse, clitoral stimulation, lesbianism, "sexual slavery," the sexual revolution, sex and age, and female sexuality.

The respondents can be simple and direct: "Clitoral orgasms make me desire intercourse." Or they can be as rhapsodic as anything out of D.H. Lawrence: "First, tension builds in my body and head, my heart beats, then I strain against my lover, then there is a second or two of absolute stillness, nonbreathing . . . Then waves, and I rock against my partner and cannot hold tight enough. It's all over my body, but especially in my abdomen and butt. Afterwards, I feel suffused with warmth and love and absolute happiness."

While praising Hite's respondents one must also praise Hite, because she asked all the right questions, all the necessary questions, which, when answered, help lead to a deeper understanding of the extraordinary complexity of female sexuality.

THE BEASTLY BEATITUDES OF BALTHAZAR B.

by J.P. Donleavy
Dell Publishing Co., Inc., 1968

Here is a sweet/sad lyrical ballad of a book. It is also bawdy in the precise sense of that word, and very, very funny. It chronicles the wanderings-through-life of Balthazar B., a wealthy and elegant vagabond looking to connect with another human soul (to be exact, a woman) but remaining always alone.

The book begins with Balthazar's babyhood, follows him through his childhood, his early school and university years, and into young manhood. He is ever naive and innocent, and getting involved in incredibly hilarious scrapes because of it. He is also devilishly attractive to women, yet he cannot, owing to various gyrations of circumstance, establish a lasting relationship with any of the women (beginning with his mother, then his nanny, then several others) with whom he falls in love.

As Candide had his Dr. Pangloss, so Balthazar B. has his guides—two exquisitely decadent voluptuaries. First there is Uncle Edouard, rakehell hunter, balloonist, explorer, sexual adventurer. Then there is school chum Beefy, vice-monger, celebrator of life, on a constant quest for ever more delicious forms of heterosexual depravity. Beefy continuously pops in and out of Balthazar's life, includes him in his bawdy doings, but never strips him of his innocence.

Donleavy is a master novelist. He offers no

cheap shots, no easy laughs or easy weeps. And anyone who has ever been alone, who has wanted and tried to find another person to be with, will find much in this novel to identify with.

THE JOY OF SEX

by Alex Comfort
Simon & Schuster, 1974

Alex Comfort asks the readers of this book to understand sex as a whole-body experience. Accordingly, he presents a rich variety of sexual possibilities as well as some useful anatomical and physiological information.

The book is divided into six sections. "Advanced Lovemaking" boils down to two rules: "One is 'don't do anything you don't really enjoy,' and the other is, 'find out your partner's needs and don't balk them if you can help it.' " From there, it's no holds barred.

The "Art of Lovemaking" section is all drawings, with short commentaries accompanying the large color pictures. "Starters" includes all the basics, from beds to foreskin to vulva. "Main Courses" is mostly positions and techniques, while "Sauces and Pickles" includes some of the more unusual sexual practices. "Problems" comprises everything from aging to venereal disease.

One drawback of the book is the stiff, in fact joyless, look of the people in the drawings—exuberance and abandon are called for (think of Picasso's erotic engravings, or the Japanese "pillow books"). Still, *The Joy of Sex* can be helpful to those looking to enrich their sex lives. It urges, rather than preaches, in a pleasant, positive way.

ON ADVANCED LOVEMAKING

This book is about love as well as sex as the title implies: you don't get high quality sex on any other basis—either you love each other before you come to want it, or, if you happen to get it, you love each other because of it, or both. No point in arguing this, but just as you can't cook without heat you can't make love without feedback (which may be the reason we say 'make love' rather than 'make sex'). Sex is the one place where we today can learn to treat people as people. Feedback means the right mixture of stop and go, tough and tender, exertion and affection. This comes by empathy and long mutual knowledge. Anyone who *expects* to get this in a first attempt with a stranger is an optimist, or a neurotic—if he does, it is what used to be called love at first sight, and isn't expendable: 'skill', or variety, are no substitutes. Also one can't teach tenderness . . . .

A little theory makes sex more interesting, more comprehensible, and less scarey—too much is a put-down, especially as you're likely to get it out of perspective and become a spectator of your own performance. If you have really troublesome hangups you need an expert to hold the mirror and go personally into what they mean—self-adhesive labels are actively unhelpful. All humans are sadistic, narcissistic, masochistic, bisexual and what have you—if you stuck on all the labels you would look like a cabin trunk. What matters is whether any of the behaviors in which you engage are bothering you or other people—if so, they are a useful pointer to what the problem is, but no more.

From The Joy of Sex

FOR YOURSELF: THE FULFILLMENT OF FEMALE SEXUALITY

by Lonnie Garfield Barbach
Doubleday & Co., 1975

For Yourself is a thoughtful, intelligent book which can help lead women with orgasmic dysfunctions to a discovery of, and a deeper understanding of, their own sexuality, and ultimately to a positive resolution to their orgasmic difficulties.

Barbach deals with many of the myths and "doublethink" that surround women's sexuality. She makes it clear that until quite recently the "experts" on women's sexuality were all men. Their descriptions of what a woman's sexual experiences are and ought to be were accepted widely if not universally as gospel. The author says, in effect, forget all the stuff you've ever heard, particularly from male experts, and pay attention to your own body, your own sexuality, where you are now.

There is detailed anatomical information as well, a thorough discussion of the physiology of sexual response and an equally thorough discussion of the psychology of sexual response. Central to what Barbach advises is the use of masturbation, principally as a way of learning about your own sexual responses, and also as a perfectly acceptable human sexual activity. She guides the reader carefully and sensitively through masturbation techniques and examines various attitudes toward masturbation.

Ultimately, this book, which discusses all facets of women's sexuality, is just as important for men who truly wish to be sensitive, responsive sex partners as it is for women who are working to overcome sex problems.

LONELY IN AMERICA

by Suzanne Gordon
Simon & Schuster, 1976

Lonely in America is a study of the topography of loneliness. Suzanne Gordon sees loneliness as a pervasive problem in our society: "Life in America has exploded, and loneliness is one main ingredient in the fall-out. What was once a philosophical problem, spoken of mainly by poets and prophets, has now become an almost permanent condition for millions of Americans, not only for the divorced but also for men and women filling singles bars and encounter groups, the adolescents running away from home or refusing to go to school, the corporate transients who move every two or three years, and the people calling suicide and crisis hot lines in search of someone to talk to."

Gordon begins with an introduction about the "Geography of Loneliness." Next, she deals with "Experiences of Loneliness," telling the stories of children, adolescents, single, divorced, and aged people. Finally, she examines "The Loneliness Business"—everything from singles bars and singles apartments to dating services, encounter groups and various psycho-spiritual trippers. Each of these dangles the carrot of true companionship or true happiness just out of the reach of lonely people.

This book doesn't make any false promises such as Read This Book And Learn How To Overcome Loneliness. It is an intelligent and solid work, much different from the squishy, sentimental ones that are flooding the market of late.

LOOKING FOR MR. GOODBAR

by Judith Rossner
Pocket Books, 1975

On the first page of this novel we learn that its heroine, Theresa Dunn, has been murdered. Then the author flashes back to Theresa's life in New York City and the inner and outer journeys that brought her to her death.

Theresa grew up in New York in an Irish-Catholic family. She had two sisters, and a brother who died in an automobile accident when he was very young. When Theresa was a child she contracted polio, which left her with a permanent limp.

She attended college in New York City and had a love affair with one of her professors, which ended sadly for her when she graduated. After college she became a schoolteacher.

In matters of sex, Theresa had a lot of old

Catholic puritanism to shake off. The more men she dated and slept with, the more she learned about her own sexuality. Accompanying her growing sexual awareness was a growing general self-awareness. She learned much about herself from seeing the kinds of men she chose to be with. She began to explore parts of her psychological self buried deep under years of repression. Her ''promiscuity'' was no carefree frolic through the sexually free landscape of the 1970s, but a painful searching for her own personal identity.

One night Theresa picked up a man in a bar, took him home with her, had sex, then tried to get him to leave. He wouldn't. A struggle followed, and he killed her. Telling the ending at the beginning doesn't ruin the book. Rossner has absolute control over her story. It's less the plot than the gritty, realistic portrait Rossner presents of a young woman's search-through-sex that makes *Looking for Mr. Goodbar* worth reading.

THE SINGLES BUSINESS

Every single or divorced person in New York City has heard of Maxwell's Plum. Even those who are only passing through Manhattan may have gone out of their way to look through the floor-to-ceiling windows that dominate the northwest corner of 64th Street and First Avenue. Equipped with a huge English-style pub bar in the center of the room, a glassed-in table area wrapping around the street corner, and a large dining room where couples can watch the action at the bar and men can invite a woman they have just picked up to an expensive and impressive meal following drinks, Maxwell's is the hottest and most elegant of the singles bars among Manhattan's East Side strip of singles gathering spots. And being jostled around the bar or waiting in line on the street outside of Maxwell's is part of being single in New York City.

After eight, however, people start arriving in cabs, on foot, or by bus. The women come in groups of two or three and the men come either alone or with a friend. Women rarely come alone to Maxwell's. Although other women can be competition, the traditional notion is that a woman alone is fair game for all unserious contenders. This discourages the lone woman from making an appearance in a singles bar. Many women today might want sex and sex only, but they don't want to appear obvious.

Once the crowd begins to grow the atmosphere changes. Being packed together around the bar along with hundreds of other people tends to loosen you up. It's easy to talk to the man or woman against whom you have been pushed by the crowd. And at Maxwell's, as at other singles bars, the action has to do with how many people are in the room. With a few drinks and a few hundred people, conversations begin.

Swingers are interested in the here and now, and so what is important is not what you do or where you come from but whether you are available for this or any other evening. One does not begin a conversation at Maxwell's with "What do you do?" or "Where do you come from?" The most important thing is to make a quick impression, be different from the hundreds of other people going in and out of the bar, so that you can get the name and number of the man or woman in whom you are interested before the crowd pushes you away or before that person leaves for the evening.

From Lonely in America

Parenting

Voices

KIDS IN YOUR LIFE

I'm neurotically attached to my six-year-old child. We're like sisters. We're best friends. We do everything together. We take baths together. We play the piano. I play with her friends. She plays with my friends. I sometimes worry about this tremendous closeness and how much I am dependent on her.

Jennifer F., married 5 years,
divorced 5 years, age 34

There are times when I've just had it with the kids. I can't deal with them effectively and there's no one I can turn to and say, "All right, you take them for a while. I'm splitting." I've got to sit there and do it. And that's about the only time I really wish I weren't single.

Bruce F., married 10 years,
separated 2 years, age 38

I'd love to raise a child. I think if I get to a certain age, maybe 35 or 40, and if I'm not in a relationship, I will consider adopting a child. I'm not clear about it. I've just begun to entertain it because I realize now this single state of mine could go on.

Sara C., age 31

I've thought of adopting a child but that has several drawbacks. First of all, I am a busy person and in order to maintain a reasonable income I would not have enough time for the child.

Sally A., age 33

It scares me to think of living without the kids. It scares me less now than it used to because I'm feeling more of a whole person. But for a long time I felt no other meaning in life except doing for my children—fixing decent meals because of them and keeping decent hours and keeping up a public image and a home. It never felt like a burden.

I have three volumes of photo albums I've kept faithfully all through the years. I don't know why. It's just always seemed important to me. People look at those books and they say, "Wow, that reflects so much love. You must have really sacrificed. You've done so much with your children, taking them on trips and everything." But it's never seemed like a sacrifice to me. It's fun.

I wasn't ready to be free and on my own. Total freedom would have frightened me. My children provided me with a refuge from my fear. They've been easy to raise. The only problems are logistical ones, which are pretty easy to solve, especially now that the kids are seven and twelve.

Lately I'm beginning to think about the freedom I'll have when the kids are gone. And I look upon that as evidence of my growth, that I can finally conceive of living without them. But the strange thing is, now that I finally feel free enough to say, "Would you like to go live with your father?" they say, "No, we kind of like your style better." And that's fine, because I have enough freedom with them. They don't cramp my style.

Martha A., married 10 years,
divorced 5 years, age 37

I'm probably going to have a child sometime soon. A woman I know has offered to have

my child and give him or her to me. She'll nurse the child but I will have primary responsibility because I'm the one who wants it. She's already got a child. I'll dig having all kinds of experiences teaching it.

Larry H., married 4 years,
separated 2 years, age 32

PARENTING ALONE

I've learned a lot about handling my children by watching a good friend interact with her kids. And sometimes she's commented, in a loving way, about some of the things I'm doing with my kids and how I could do better. I also got involved in a single-parent group at school. We met twice a month for almost a year. We talked about the problems we had as single adults with children—how you cope with getting your own space and your own time. The P.T.A. sponsored it. It was very helpful, especially on the mechanics.

Bruce F., married 10 years,
separated 2 years, age 38

I think it's easier since I've been divorced although I regret that they're not exposed to a father a lot. And they're subjected to my moods, having no recourse. If I'm feeling lousy there's no one else they can turn to, and that's kind of sad. I look with longing at all the intact families in the neighborhood. I think how great it is and feel envy, not for myself so much as for the children. I look at men doing things with their sons and expressing warmth to their daughters. I think that's so important.

Still, I have a fair amount of confidence in the way I am raising them. I like having a free hand and not getting static. My husband would always say, "You're too hard on Linda and too easy on Rob." He was always harping on this and I know there's some truth to it. But I think I'm dealing with it O.K. It's sort of a trip being the sole authority.

Martha A., married 10 years,
divorced 5 years, age 37

THE OTHER PARENT

My six-year-old daughter does not remember the time when her daddy and mommy lived in the same house. She does ask about it and we tell her about it and she's completely at peace with the idea that there's a mommy's house and a daddy's house. She's never seen us quarrel.

She would like me to get married again. She wants babies. She says it's lonely in the house. She liked it very much one time when I had a man living here for a long while. When he left she said, "Mommy, just get any man to stay here. I can't go to bed without a man in the house." I felt really badly about that. Ideally, she would like me to marry her father. She talks about it all the time.

When she visits him he's really nice to her. Verbally he wants her all the time and he says he loves her. But she really doesn't fit into his social life. So there will be long periods when he won't see her. And he rarely pays child support.

I have to admit his behavior doesn't surprise me. When I first met him he was hiding out from a desertion charge against him. He's sort of a rogue. He's very glamorous, charming, extroverted, and absolutely immoral.

Jennifer F., married 5 years,
divorced 5 years, age 34

One was seven and the other two. The older child was pretty depressed about the situation. And it was very sad. My husband would come and visit and then we would take him to the plane. She would cry on the way home. But, eventually, he came often enough that she became used to it. It's worked itself out pretty well. The younger one just grew up thinking that this type of household was normal.

Also, we did have a man friend at the time who was around a lot. I think he helped my kids over the hump.

Martha A., married 10 years,
divorced 5 years, age 37

Since I have custody I make the major decisions about my kids' lives. I do give my wife some option about it, particularly about vacations and things like that. I try to be somewhat fair in spite of my anger towards her.

Bruce F., married 10 years,
separated 2 years, age 38

I was having a pretty hard time of it in the period right after our separation. I had to leave the house. I now had to support two households. I didn't have easy access to my kids. And I was under attack by my wife's lawyer.

The immediate feeling was, I must have done something horrible to have all of this heaped on me. But then someone at Parents Without Partners suggested I go to a meeting of Fathers United and that has made a big difference in my life.

The main purpose of Fathers United is to show the man that there are ways of getting

a more equitable settlement concerning the children. I thought this was great. Here was a whole group of fathers who have the point of view that they can fight back and they can win. They can do something about the system which still is biased against fathers.

Eventually I met some guys from my town and I said, "Look, we need a chapter like this in our jurisdiction." We started calling around and in two months we found 50 people who were interested. And that's how we got started. We now have about 200 fathers. We hold meetings twice a month. There's usually a presentation by an attorney. We've covered topics such as visitation rights and divided custody. And we listen to specific problems men are having and we try to suggest strategies right there. Men who have been in similar circumstances will share their experiences.

Gordon F., married 8 years,
divorced 3 years, age 48

The Baby

MARGARET DRABBLE

I left hospital in a taxi on the tenth day with Octavia in my arms and Lydia by my side. I was excited at the thought of getting home and having my baby to myself, but the cold of the outside air must have startled her, for she began to scream and screech violently in the taxi, and when we got home I did not quite know what to do. In hospital she had always been so quiet and sweet. I laid her down in her basket, but the mattress was a different shape from the hospital cot, and she looked strange and uncomfortable and screamed all the more fiercely. She looked odd, too, in her own Viyella nighties, after the regulation garments she had worn all her life until that afternoon. She went on and on crying and I began to think that she would never adapt to real life. Lydia was getting almost as worried as I was, and after a while she said, as we both sat miserably and watched this small furious person, 'Why don't you feed her? That would shut her up, wouldn't it?'

I looked at my watch; it was half past four.

'It's not time to feed her yet,' I said. 'In hospital, we had to feed them on the dot .'

'Oh,' said Lydia, 'half an hour one way or the other can't make much difference.'

'Don't you think so?' I said. 'But then she'll wake half an hour early at the next feed, and the next, and the next, and then what will I do?'

'It wouldn't matter, would it?'

'I don't know. I somehow feel things would get all muddled and never get straight again. She was good and reasonable in hospital. And then she'll get confused, and how will she ever know when it's night time? How will she ever learn that it's night?'

'I should feed her,' said Lydia. 'It looks to me

as though she's going to have a fit.'

I didn't think she would have a fit, but I couldn't stand the sound of her crying, so I picked her out and fed her, and she became quiet at once, and fell asleep afterwards looking as though her mattress and nightdress were very comfortable after all. On the other hand, she did wake half an hour early at the next feed, and went on and on waking earlier, until we worked right back round the clock, for the truth was that she never went four hours but only three and a half. Looking back on it, it doesn't seem to matter at all, but it seemed very important at the time, I remember. It took her ages, moreover, to learn about night and day, and in the end I concluded that they had been giving her secret bottles in the night at the hospital.

However, on the whole, things worked out very well. I had a subsidized home help to begin with, and after a fortnight or so this woman whom Lydia had discovered, an amiable fat lady named Mrs. Jennings, came in two days a week while I dashed off to the library between feeds. Mrs. Jennings adored babies, and I found that all her chat about little darling tiny thingies, and where's her little tootsie wootsies, fell quite naturally and indeed gratefully upon my ears. I very shortly gave up feeding Octavia myself, as to my amazement I found the process quite infuriating and nerve-wracking: I stuck it for six weeks, hoping that as the more modern books said it would become a pleasure, or at least less of a drag, and the baby certainly seemed to enjoy it, but in the end I could stand it no longer and gave up. I didn't find the act itself disgusting, or anything like that, but the consequences were extremely messy; I grew frantic at the way my clothes got covered in milk,

I certainly had not anticipated such wreathing, dazzling gaiety of affection from her whenever I happened to catch her eye.

and in fact those six weeks have had a permanent effect on my life, for now I am as fussy as Clare about dirt, and am forever washing my clothes before they need it, sending things to the cleaners when I can't afford it, and paying secret nocturnal visits to the launderette. Also, despite evidence to the contrary, I could never believe that there was really anything there, that the baby was really getting anything at all to drink. What the eye doesn't see, I don't believe in, and the first time I gave her a bottle and watched the milk-level descending, ounce by careful ounce, I was overcome with relief, and I think I counted that as the first real meal of her life.

Octavia was an extraordinarily beautiful child. Everyone said so, in shops and on buses and in the park, wherever we went. I took her to Regent's Park as often as I could face getting the pram up and down in the lift. It was a tolerable summer, and we both got quite brown. I was continually amazed by the way in which I could watch for hours nothing but the small movements of her hands, and the fleeting expressions of her face. She was a very happy child, and once she learned to smile, she never stopped; at first she would smile at anything, at parking meters and dogs and strangers, but as she grew older she began to favour me, and nothing gave me more delight than her evident preference. I suppose I had not really expected her to dislike and resent me from birth, though I was quite prepared for resentment to follow later on, but I certainly had not anticipated such wreathing, dazzling gaiety of affection from her whenever I happened to catch her eye. Gradually I began to realize that she liked me, that she had no option to liking me, and that unless I took great pains to alienate her she would go on liking me, for a couple of years at least. It was very pleasant to receive such uncritical love, because it left me free to bestow love; my kisses were met by small warm rubbery unrejecting cheeks and soft dovey mumblings of delight.

Indeed, it must have been in expectation of this love that I had insisted upon having her, or rather refrained from not having her: something in me had clearly known before I did that there would be compensations. I was not of course treated to that phrase which greets all reluctant married mothers, 'I bet you wouldn't be without her now,' so often repeated after the event, in the full confidence of nature, because I suppose people feared I might turn on them and say, Yes I certainly would, which would be mutually distressing for questioner and me. And in many ways I thought that I certainly would prefer to be without her, as one might reasonably prefer to lack beauty or intelligence or riches, or any other such sources of mixed blessing and pain. Things about life with a baby drove me into frenzies of weeping several times a week, and not only having milk on my clean jerseys. As so often in life, it was impossible to choose, even theoretically, between advantage and disadvantage, between profit and loss: I was up quite unmistakably against No Choice. So the best one could do was to put a good face on it, and to avoid adding to the large and largely discussed number of sad warnings that abounded in the part of the world that I knew. I managed very well, and the general verdict was Extraordinary Rosamund, she really seems happy, she must have really wanted one after all.

From *The Millstone* by Margaret Drabble

Books

MOMMA: THE SOURCEBOOK FOR SINGLE MOTHERS

edited by Karol Hope and Nancy Young
New American Library, 1976

Sometimes we need more than just technical advice, we need to hear people who've experienced what we're experiencing tell about their lives, tell how they've made it, or are making it, through the briarpatch. This book is that kind of book, the personal stories of many, many single mothers. It's less like a manual and more like warm conversations with good friends.

The book is divided into seven sections, each identifying significant aspects of single motherhood. "Nobody Else Knows What We're All About"gathers stories that provide a vivid picture of just what the single-mother life style is all about. "Rites of Passage" deals with separation and divorce. "Doing It/ Moving On" includes the stories of women after they've left their partners and are setting up brand new lives. "Kids and Us" shares women's experiences raising their children without partners. "Co-Parenting" deals with parents' efforts to share responsibility for the children even after the split. "Men" deals with issues like single fatherhood and how men relate to single mothers. And "Momma, The Organization for Single Mothers" gives a history of the group, founded in 1972, that generated this book.

Though the book comprises personal anecdotes and stories, that doesn't mean it is short on good, concrete advice. In fact, it's loaded with bits of useful information about such things as how to get welfare, getting into college, child care, dealing with sibling rivalry, handling money, enforcing court orders, and

more. The stories give the practical information a flesh-and-blood context, making it all seem so much more possible and real.

EAT ALONE WITH YOUR CHILDREN AND LIKE IT

by Susan Minard and Paula M. Berka
Mynabird Publishing Company,
20 Shoshone Place, Portola Valley, CA 94025,
1976

Having no partner to share the household responsibilities is tough on the single parent. One of the most demanding tasks is meal preparation. Here's a book that aims to lighten the burden of the single-parent cook and, perhaps, take off some of the emotional charge that can often change a pleasant family time into a battle royale.

Of course it's not just recipes the single parent is wanting. It's menus, too, that he or she needs to help eliminate much of that time-consuming, brain-busting planning. The book serves well on that count, presenting menus and recipes together—each menu item is accompanied by its recipe. The emphasis falls equally on dishes that are relatively quick and easy to prepare, balanced nutrition, and variety.

Beyond recipes and menus, there is useful information on economical shopping, some basic nutritional guidance, and a nice chapter on "Peaceful Table Relations"—nothing particularly profound, but some pleasant and helpful sharing of thoughts. A chapter entitled "Entertainment Ideas or How to Keep the Kids Busy in the Kitchen While You're Sitting by the Fire with a Date" provides recipes for hors d'oeuvres and drinks that kids can make mostly or entirely by themselves.

LONELINESS AT THE TABLE

Some reasons why single parents feel lonely at the table:

1. Children are apt to make uncomplimentary remarks about a food you slaved over all afternoon, and you would like to force feed your unwarranted critics. If another adult were present he or she would probably rally to your defense with, "You don't have to eat it but don't spoil it for the rest of us who happen to like creamed sweetbreads on toast."

2. Even if the kids like what you're serving, the ungrateful little wretches will often sit at the table and stuff their faces without telling you the fried chicken is great. Adults are usually more vocal in praising the cook, and the constant cook's ego needs gratification now and then. . . .

3: The single parent also lacks another adult to aid in stopping sibling squabbles which may also indicate a need for more attention.

4. Table conversation between one parent and children can range from almost complete silence with only an occasional, "Pass the mustard," to bedlam where each child wants to tell the parent a blow by blow account of a James Bond movie. When two adults sit at the table, the conversation gains another mature viewpoint, providing topics not limited to the strictly juvenile but, we hope, of interest to all. Children have been observed to even listen to what adults are saying and to ask questions and offer opinions.

Ways to overcome aloneness:

1. Get together once a week with another family, either the single or two parent kind. Adults may want to eat at a separate table if the children are good friends and enjoy having their own party. Entertaining adults, in addition to providing you with mature conversation, will boost your self-image as a cook when friends praise your dinner.

2. Make a break with traditions. It is especially painful during holiday meals the first year after a divorce or death of a mate. Do something different; start new traditions and include the kids in your planning. Try new foods. If you always went to Aunt Hester's for Easter, invite her to your egg hunt. Have a midnight supper on Christmas Eve with friends and their children in front of the fireplace.

3. Vary the monotony of everyday meals, too, by changing locations. Eat on the porch, patio or on the lawn in summer. Go to a park for dinner or for breakfast. Move your dinner in front of the TV for special programs of interest to all. (A steady diet of TV news with dinner can be depressing.)

4. Ask the children about changes at the table. Would it be fun to buy drippy candles and put them in wine bottles to light the table in winter—saving energy and making wax-covered bottles? Let the kids take turns lighting and extinguishing the flame. Make new mats and napkins from inexpensive no-iron fabric; even boys like to fringe mats. Grow flowers with your children for the table. Let them pick and arrange using different containers: colored bottles, teapots, brandy or sherbet glasses. Make paper or cloth flowers for winter color. Burn incense at the table, especially if you've cooked an odoriforous vegetable. Unless your children live in blue jeans get dressed up and dress up the table with your best dishes and cutlery on a Sunday.

From *Eat Alone With Your Children and Like It*

If you're a single parent looking for kitchen help, you might want to pop $7.95 for this book; it's cheaper than a live-in cook.

BACHELOR FATHERHOOD

by Michael McFadden
Walker and Company, 1974

In the introduction to his book, Michael McFadden writes, "Over the years I've lived alone, I've lived with male roommates, lived with various women, lived with a wife, and lived with a wife and children. I like my present setup best. I have the advantages of being single and many of the joys of family life." McFadden is a single father living with his three children.

This is a positive, breezy, anecdotal book about single parenthood, male division. Apparently McFadden had few if any doubts about his ability and suitability to raise his kids on his own. So he just went right ahead and did it, convincing his former wife it was a sound decision, restructuring his business life so he could be at home most of the time.

Though the book contains some useful bits of practical advice on housework, cooking, and related subjects, it's more of a pep talk than a guidebook. McFadden is wholly and cheerfully in the corner of any father who wants to have custody of his kids, and sounds nary a negative note about bachelor fatherhood.

For those who want to roll up their sleeves and grapple with the really profound, difficult personal and social issues single fatherhood raises, other books will serve better. But for those who'd like their spirits lifted a bit, an affectionate kick in the seat of the morale, this book may be just the right boot.

THE SINGLE PARENT EXPERIENCE

by Carol Klein
Walker and Company, 1973

Single parenthood is a serious and growing phenomenon, not simply because marriages are breaking up all the time, but also because many single women who become pregnant are choosing to have and keep their babies with-

out marrying the father, and because never-married people are being allowed to adopt children in ever greater numbers.

Klein surveys all the interesting contours of single parenthood: homosexual parents, single parenthood as social protest, single parents living communally, interracial adoption, and more. And besides presenting the sociology of the phenomenon, she examines the inner workings, both technical and psychological, as well: loneliness, dating and sex problems for the single parent, legal issues in private adoption, tax problems, day care centers, whose name goes on the birth certificate, and many more.

The message of Klein's book is clear: More and more people are beginning to separate the state of parenthood from the state of marriage, a fundamental reversal of a traditional attitude which will surely have extensive repercussions in the entire society. Klein doesn't plead the case for single parents, she merely presents it, with the implicit demand that it be taken seriously.

A GUIDE FOR SINGLE PARENTS

by Kathryn Hallett
Celestial Arts, 1974

Most single parents got that way through a loss—death, divorce, separation. And along with that loss, something was added: increased parental responsibilities. Both the loss of a partner and the sudden doubling of responsibilities are crises in peoples' lives, crises they must confront and resolve if they're to lead meaningful, happy lives outside and inside the home. Kathryn Hallett proposes Transactional Analysis techniques for getting through to the other side.

TA identifies three ego states that we carry around with us at all times. There is the Parent, an amalgam, really, of all the "thou-shalts" and "thou-shalt-nots" we learned from our parents when we were young. There is the Child, us when we were young, with all our fears and confusions still intact. And there is the Adult, a kind of fully integrated, wise person with a broad understanding that can embrace both the Parent and the Child. According to TA theory, we shift from one to another of these ego states all the time. The key to a healthy personality and to healthy relationships is not necessarily to get rid of Parent and Child, but to allow the free and appropriate flow of feelings among all three ego states.

Hallett suggests that it's crucial for single parents to get in touch with the Child state in themselves and open up the flow from it to the other states. When parents can really touch those childhood tender spots, they'll understand themselves better and likely have a lot more patience and a lot deeper compassion for what their children are going through.

For people suffering through the continuing repercussions of separation, *A Guide for Single Parents* might provide some good help.

WHO WILL RAISE THE CHILDREN?

by James A. Levine
J.B. Lippincott Company, 1976

Nobody needs to make a case for a mother to gain custody of her children after a divorce; it's *presumed* the mother will get the kids. But the message we've been getting in newspaper and magazine articles and TV talk shows these past few years is that more and more fathers *want* custody of their children. Every single father who functions successfully as a full-time parent helps build the case for fathering in general. James Levine joins the cause with this book.

Levine quotes some legal scholars on the "maternal presumption" who say that regardless of laws that stipulate that the best interests of the child rather than parental sex will determine custody, "due to the mystique of motherhood, the mother has the advantage and, except in the most unusual cases, will be awarded custody when she seeks it, unless there is a strong showing of unfitness or abandonment . . . in effect many of the decisions tacitly imply that the father's claim to custody as against the mother's is slightly, if any, better than that of an utter stranger."

By examining the life situations of many single fathers who are making it quite well with their children, Levine assembles a mov-

ing argument in favor of the nurturing father. Whether or not a book like this can have any strong, immediate impact on a system that heavily favors the mother, it is an important document in the movement toward a more human vision of fathers, of seeing that they can be loving, caring, competent parents—neither Dagwood Bumstead nor Attila the Hun.

PART-TIME FATHER

by Edith Atkin and Estelle Rubin
The Vanguard Press, Inc., 1976

There is a special ring of hell reserved for those parents—traditionally fathers—who are separated from their children by divorce. The real substance (and hence the real joys as well as the drudgery) of parenting is the day-to-day being with kids. When that is taken away, absent parents come to feel like "Uncle Daddy" or "Aunt Mommy"—a more-or-less pleasant, amusing, fun, but nonessential relative.

Of course, the removed parent doesn't become nonessential. But his or her role is so vague, his or her real worth so hard to discern, that the feelings of uselessness can become overpowering. Then, too, conflict with an ex-mate is likely to go on. The difficulty of part-time parenting is aggravated enormously by continuing tensions between ex-partners.

Here's a book that seeks to help the part-time parent, in particular the part-time father, since it is the father, still, who is normally amputated from the family in divorces. *Part-Time Father* is a guide that covers many important issues from the styles of visits to split custody to father's new wife. The authors discuss the special problems of being with very young children and with adolescents. They talk about what to do on special occasions, how to structure weekends, how to talk about ex-partners.

Thorough in the range of subjects it covers, *Part-Time Father* examines no subject deeply. It's an introductory course rather than an advanced one. Still, it is an intelligent and compassionate book about a complex and emotionally charged subject.

Recreation

Voices

GOING OUT

I go to movies by myself and I go to bars by myself and it doesn't scare me. Going with somebody to a movie has nothing to do with how much I enjoy it because when I'm watching a movie I am by myself. The other person has nothing to do with the movie. If I think the movie is funny I sit there and laugh. I don't have to have somebody sitting beside me to help me laugh at the movie. Sometimes I miss having somebody to talk about the movie with afterwards, but I guess if I really felt an irresistible urge to talk about the movie I would run up to someone right after the movie and say, "Hey, what did you think of that movie?"

Cindy W., age 34

I had a big fear of doing things by myself. Like I couldn't go and eat in a restaurant by myself. I wouldn't go to a movie by myself. I started by going out alone during the day. I'd take walks out by the marsh or go over to the ocean. One night I wanted to go to a movie. I couldn't find anyone to go with me. So I said, "Well, I'll have to go by myself." And I went and I sat in the theater and I looked around. There must have been about six other women in there by themselves. I figured it was O.K.

Now I feel really comfortable doing all sorts of things on my own. And when I see couples I don't feel badly that I'm alone. I like to sit and watch people. I know enough people now that if I want company, I can find it.

*Holly H., married 3 years,
divorced 3 years, age 29*

I like to do a lot of things by myself. Since I take part in team sports, I do spend a fair amount of time with others. But I don't necessarily know the people I'm playing ball with. So that can be pretty much a solitary thing for me, too, even though I'm doing it with somebody else.

*Patrick R., married 4 years,
divorced 2 years, age 34*

I don't usually like doing things alone, but when I do them, like going to see a movie, it's really very satisfying. It's a whole different experience seeing a movie alone. After the movie's over you can reflect on it deeply.

Jesse F., age 34

I like to see movies alone. I don't always feel comfortable doing that—it still feels awkward to me. But I like to do it because I don't need to carry on a dialogue about the film afterward. I can let myself be immersed in the film and go up or down after the film totally on my own. Like *Adele H.* made me sad. I don't remember why, but I remember walking out and it was a rainy day that just fit the gloominess I felt. I really let myself be transported by that emotion for as long as I had to go with it and I really felt satisfied afterward. Whereas if I had been with someone else I would have had to cut that off very abruptly. I would have felt, "Well, I'm not going to foist this on somebody else. I'll just cut it off." I prefer not doing that. I can ride with the emotion much better if I'm by myself.

*Donna R., married 2 years,
divorced 7 years, age 30*

STAYING HOME

Occasionally I need to have a weekend to myself, to clean, to read, to do a project. At the end I feel very rejuvenated. Then once more I am happy to be around people.

Ruth G., age 46

I love to watch sports on TV. I do my embroidery while I'm doing that. I couldn't waste time just sitting. I'm usually invited out Saturday evenings to dinner at my son's or at friends'. I go to church every Sunday morning. Then, Sunday afternoons I go on walks. I don't know. It doesn't take much to make me happy.

Eleanor M., married 32 years,
widowed 10 years, age 73

I like to drink by myself. It makes me feel good. I sometimes think I should give it up, but I'm drinking less and less so I'm not worried. And I really enjoy it too much to give it up. I know I could probably get just as high on nothing if I wanted to. But I like the alcohol. I drink Scotch because I think it's better for me though I don't really know that.

Ellen B., married 22 years,
divorced 3 years, age 58

I enjoy celebrating my birthday alone. I buy myself something that I like, for instance, a special bottle of wine or a new shirt. I wish myself a good birthday. Why not?

George P., age 25

I never put my guitar in its case. I'll take it up and play it five or six times a day. A lot of my feelings come out through that.

Jesse F., age 34

One of my favorite things to do is to go to a bookstore and buy a new book or a bunch of magazines. Then I'll go home, take a bubble bath, put on a clean T-shirt, and get into bed. I love to be in bed with my books.

Sara C., age 31

I like to laugh by myself. When I notice myself doing something unusual or funny, it can make me laugh.

Mark B., age 28

ENTERTAINING

I never entertain in the broad sense of the word. I would never have a party. That's a very foreign experience to me. I like to entertain one person or two. Four would be the limit. A larger party would be out of my experience. I don't even like to go to parties, let alone give them. I watched an acquaintance prepare a brunch. He had to go through so much nervous stuff. I wasn't sure what the purpose of going through it was. This may sound ridiculously rational as if

everything I do has to have a justifiable outcome. But I just don't get off on bringing together a bunch of people. Having a crowd only makes me feel self-conscious.

Donna R., married 2 years,
divorced 7 years, age 30

The kind of entertaining I typically do now is with single parents who come with their kids for dinner.

Bruce F., married 10 years,
separated 2 years, age 38

My entertaining is spontaneous. I'll call up someone and arrange a potluck on the spot. Our parties usually end up with everybody sitting on the floor talking in small groups or playing Scrabble and Monopoly. We're into board games. We'll just sit around and scream at each other all night about Park Place or Boardwalk.

Sally A., age 33

I give two big parties every year and small dinner parties about once every two weeks. I usually let people bring stuff. I don't call it a potluck. I keep it very free because my friends know I don't have as much money as they do. I'm not a good cook anyhow. And so at my parties usually the guests do everything.

Jennifer F., married 5 years,
divorced 5 years, age 34

TRAVEL

I find that when I travel alone it opens up a lot of possibilities. People are curious why you are alone. They might feel sorry for you. They might want to enter into a relationship with you.

George P., age 25

The first time I traveled alone I felt the same kind of anxiety as I had when I first got divorced. "How do I do this?" "Who am I in this role?" "What do I do next?" I was filled with a lot of worry about my competence to do it and just the unknown things that might come up.

But when I started traveling a lot as part of my job and found that I could do it, I felt terrific. Especially about the little things like reading a map. I had never even looked at a map in my life. I really expected the men in my life to get me from one place to another. I was very traditional in that sense. When I found I was able to do that stuff there was a feeling of power over things, which seems a good thing to have.

Traveling as a vacation is different. I don't feel as comfortable with that yet. It doesn't have structure. You have to be more creative and a bit more outgoing. But there's something very positive about it because it's a pure experience and it's yours. It can be very rich because you don't bounce it off somebody.

I traveled to Canada and back about a year ago in my car. I camped out, slept in my car, stuff like that. I had never done anything like that before. I remember the first time I pulled into a campground and set up my gear. The next day I was so elated by the sheer doing of it I was singing. I said to myself, "My God, what a wonderful thing. I can do it."

Donna R., married 2 years,
divorced 7 years, age 30

I'll go to a hotel and nobody knows where I am. I'll have dinner and walk around the place and feel perfectly comfortable. It's fun to be in a totally different environment and meet new people and not have anybody else help me make decisions. It makes me feel like an independent woman.

Cindy W., age 24

I go down to the beach. I have a drum and I drink and I play my drum and I sing about my life. That's really nice. It's a way of letting the energy go through me. It really clears things out. I wouldn't call it music. It's just something fun to do.

I also like to swim in the ocean. It's really beautiful to do that and I like the danger. If there are any sharks waiting out there, that doesn't bother me at all. I enjoy that fear. I really need that challenge. I think living without a little bit of danger is very flat.

Ellen B., married 22 years,
divorced 3 years, age 58

The year I retired I went on a cruise all by myself. Everybody is so nice to you when you're alone. So many people asked me to dine with them. I think if I had been traveling with somebody, I would have had fewer invitations.

Eleanor M., married 32 years,
widowed 10 years, age 73

A Solo Weekend

JOYCE MAYNARD

A couple of years back, when I lived at the end of a dirt road in New Hampshire, with the nearest neighbor half a mile away, a December blizzard left me snowed in for three days—alone.

By the time the snow stopped falling, it had piled up to where the windows started and had drifted against the door.

Then the rains came and turned to ice on the power lines, weighing them down until they broke.

Then the phone went dead.

The car wouldn't start, but even if it had, there would have been no getting up the hill into town.

At first, with not much besides half a dozen eggs in the refrigerator, and no lights, and no heat, and no water, I felt trapped. But once I'd got the fires going and melted some snow, and made a stack of pancakes on top of the wood stove, a good relaxed feeling set in.

Nobody was going to call and no mail was going to come and there was no way I could get the electric typewriter going, and it was going to stay that way for a while.

I couldn't get out and the rest of the world could not get in. An atom bomb could have dropped on Nebraska and I wouldn't have known it.

So I lit the oil lamps and read Sherlock Holmes and took out a harmonica I'd been given sometime before and never learned to play. I finished knitting a shawl I'd started two years earlier and wrote a couple of letters and painted my kitchen floor red. I may have spoken to myself once or twice, but I didn't hear another human voice for three days.

On the fourth day, I heard the snow plows coming up the road and then the refrigerator and the water pump began to make a racket and the record player and the lights came on—all at once—and a friend drove 'round to jump the battery in my car. A few hours later I was in the grocery story buying vegetables and three days' worth of newspapers.

A lot of people in the city find themselves alone on weekends and end up feeling miserable about that. It seems to me they might do better not fighting it so hard.

Listening to a good concert with a friend or dancing until 3 o'clock on Saturday morning can be a splendid way to pass a Friday night. But sometimes it is nice to see absolutely no one, to go nowhere.

So every once in a while I snow myself in for the weekend. From Friday night to Monday morning, I just decide to be alone.

It's a good idea to lay in supplies before the end of the week and get one's chores done. So I do the laundry and clean out the refrigerator. I buy flowers and candles and good soap and vegetables and fresh coffee beans.

For the price of the movie or play I won't be attending, I might get myself a book or a fine drawing pen or a purple leotard or just a nice cup and saucer for my tea. And if I'm wanting to revel in a certain pleasantly melancholy feeling, I may buy a bottle of white rum and a Dolly Parton record.

Once or twice I have seen, reprinted in magazines, the schedules followed by the frequenters of California spas, with every hour accounted for and every activity dictated, down to the musical selections one should play while doing situps, and the books (usually those of an unthreateningly inspirational nature) that one might read during Rest Hour.

Personal tastes differing as they do, this seems a mistake. So I'll just mention how I sometimes fill my 60 free weekend hours, and

The restorative benefits that come from two days taking care of nothing but one's own self are undeniable.

leave it at that.

A long bath in a dark room, with a record on, maybe, seems like the best way to begin on Friday night, and the experience is particularly fine if one fills the tub with herbs.

It can be nice to watch the late movie afterward, but I like best to keep the television off for the weekend and give my senses something of a rest. I do listen to records on my solitary weekends, but I try not to play them in the casual way I often do at other times—as background music for washing dishes or paying bills.

Something should probably be said here about the telephone. Preferring my weekends of retreat to be as uninterrupted as I can make them, I try to ignore the phone altogether, but I know that it's very difficult for a lot of people to hear a phone ringing and not answer it. Probably those are the same people who—for once in their lives—should not run to pick up the receiver at the sound of the bell.

For those who would be tormented by the thought that the call they miss might just be the call announcing the inheritance of legacy they never knew existed, it should be pointed out that determined callers try again and that plenty of phone calls are missed, anyway, when one goes out.

Some exercise is called for, I think, during one's weekend alone—if not for the pure joy of the running, or the yoga, or the side bends, then for the deferred gains of a more mundane level to be had from the flatter stomach or trimmer waist that follow. Especially if one is prone to feelings of guilt about long hours spent taking baths and giving one's self pedicures, the feeling at day's end, of faintly aching muscles, can provide a sense that one has put in the day's requisite suffering.

And because the old work ethic dies hard, one might perform some long-deferred and not hugely taxing chore like polishing the silverware or sorting out the kind of messy drawer which has come to be so embarrassing that one has simply given up on wearing socks. I am also a duster of shelves on my solitary weekends, mainly out of love for the smell of lemon furniture polish.

Most of the activities I perform in these times, though, are marginally self-improving, or purely self-indulgent. I may put myself to the task of drawing a self-portrait or memorizing a poem.

I am always meaning to read Montaigne's essays or embark on a study of European history on some weekend alone. Usually, though, I end up reading Agatha Christie, or baking bread.

Once, when I had a Sunday to myself, I dyed my hair red. That was not a good idea, but bringing about some slightly less radical change in one's appearance—like putting on a coat of nail polish or losing a couple of pounds—can give a sense of purpose to the weekend, for goal-oriented types.

It may be unlikely that when one shows up at one's job on Monday morning one's co-workers will burst out with admiring exclamations on the order of "what have you done to yourself!" But the restorative benefits that come from two days taking care of nothing but one's own self are undeniable.

More than that, though, there are internal benefits coming from a weekend spent "snowed-in," in a city apartment, that make the digestion of this Big Apple they keep telling us about a good deal easier.

From the *New York Times*

Books

THE UNIVERSAL BASEBALL ASSOCIATION, J. HENRY WAUGH, PROP.

by Robert Coover
New American Library, 1968

Henry Waugh is a 54-year-old accountant who lives alone. Henry Waugh plays baseball. Beyond that, he is the statistician for the entire league. And the historian. And the creator. The Universal Baseball Association exists on his kitchen table and in his mind and heart.

Henry discovered early on that what he liked most about real baseball wasn't the play, but the statistics. So he invented a game of his own based on complicated probability tables. He invented teams. He invented players and managers. And soon enough, the Universal Baseball Association was living and breathing inside Henry. Players have individual personalities. Things happen off the field as well as in the game. Old players die, new ones come up from the minors. Sometimes there are tragedies—from the Extraordinary Occurrences Chart.

This game of Henry's, begun as a leisurely pastime, begins to consume him. He misses work, his mind shifts into and out of UBA scenarios—before a game in the locker room, the roar of the crowd at a home run, players drinking beer after the game. The death of one young player throws Henry into a deep depression. He quits his job, goes through the motions of the rest of the season, writes its history in volume LVI of the UBA official chronicles. He tries to revitalize himself and the game by teaching it to a friend, but it doesn't work out, his friend doesn't share his passion.

Still, the UBA continues. It's clearly Henry's whole life. By the end of this book, realities so thoroughly intermingle that J. Henry Waugh has disappeared entirely into the game.

THE PLEASURE BOOK

by Julius Fast
Stein and Day, 1975

For most of us the chief pleasures in life aren't dramatic extravaganzas but simple, ordinary-seeming delights. That's one message we get from Julius Fast's *The Pleasure Book*, in which 75 people explain just what it is that gives them those moments of exquisite pleasure—escape from the routine and the humdrum.

Many people report that those moments are moments spent alone. Sylvia reexperiences her whole childhood by climbing up into her old treehouse. Chris loves to contemplate colors. Eric forages for wild foods. Bert mows the lawn in the nude. Alex meditates. Barry goes fly-fishing. Barbara sits outdoors alone at night to listen, look, and feel.

Not all the pleasures chronicled in this book are solitary ones. Rod and Al crash parties; Fast likes to be massaged; Jan, Rob, and Sarah like to play games from their childhood days. And a few of the pleasures involve some drama, even some danger. Jules shoots rapids in an inner tube. Jenny is a balloonist. Carl flies a sailplane.

Besides being a resource book that might turn you on to new pleasures, *The Pleasure Book* is a convincing statement that the central ingredient in true enjoyment isn't the exotic nature of the activity, but the wholehearted, unabashed involvement of the doer.

HIDING OUT

"When I was seventeen," Rita tells me, "I ran away from home and went into hiding." Laughing at my surprise, she adds, "I didn't go very far or stay very long. Twenty-four hours, to be exact, and I left a note telling my parents I was visiting a friend."

"Were you?"

"No, I was in hiding. It's one of my favorite pleasures. When everything piles up to the point where I just can't cope, I go into hiding. That first time I was having trouble at school and a boy friend had just walked out on me. My family and friends were rubbing me raw. I had saved up about fifty dollars from babysitting, and I checked into one of San Francisco's very classy hotels.

"I had a wonderful room overlooking the bay, and once I unpacked I took a long, leisurely bath, all scented and bubbly, then got into a caftan."

"And you were all alone?"

"That's exactly what was so wonderful. I did my nails and sprawled on the bed with some movie magazines I had bought. I watched the late show and the late, late show on TV—I couldn't ever get away with that at home. And then I slept away the morning and had breakfast in bed—it was a real fantasy trip, the way Jean Harlow used to do it in the old movies. I just loafed away twenty-four hours, and when it was over I felt completely refreshed—one day was enough to do it, that time."

"You say that time. Were there others?"

"Oh, yes. I still do it when things pile up and threaten to overwhelm me. I just duck out, wherever I am, disappear, and check into the classiest, handsomest hotel around. Sometimes a place like the Fairmont in San Francisco is perfect— that is, the old part. The rooms are so large, the ceilings so high, there's such a sense of luxury. I could never afford it on a regular basis, but every once in a while I can revel in it . . . .

"Luxury is part of the pleasure, and so is pampering myself." She adds, "I guess it's just another escape, another way of leaving everyone behind. I put away all my problems, and just luxuriate in the lavishness of it all."

"Do you ever hide out for longer than a day?"

"My limit is twenty-four hours." Very seriously, she explains, "You see, if it's for one night and at rare intervals, I can afford just about any hotel in the world. If I stayed longer I'd worry about how much I was spending, but a one-night stay, even with room service and all the extra goodies, rarely comes to over a hundred dollars, even in the most posh place. And it's all the more intense because it's only for a night. You don't get a chance, not for one minute, to get bored.

"Oh, I've done it sometimes when I have some extra money to play with, but most often I do it when the situation is bad, when things are closing in and I have to get my head on straight again. It puts everything back into perspective, and it refreshes me absolutely!"

From *The Pleasure Book*

STRING FIGURES AND HOW TO MAKE THEM

by Caroline Furness Jayne
Dover Publications, 1962

Say you're trapped on a desert island with plenty of food and water and a single piece of string. Or you've finished dinner, have no plans for the evening, TV's lousy, and as your eyes wander aimlessly around the room you notice a piece of wrapping twine on the coffee table. Or . . . well, enough. The point is, a piece of string can provide a lot of entertainment.

Most of us played a simple game of "Cat's Cradle" when we were kids—making a figure by looping string around our hands just so, then having a friend make the next figure by removing the string in just the right way, and so on. Well, the game of "Cat's Cradle" is quite a venerable one, with roots in the remote past. It's been played by countless peoples who have handed it down as a part of their culture. Many of the figures that have been created are amazing in their complexity and beauty. And there are many, many figures you can make without a partner.

String Figures and How to Make Them is everything-you-always-wanted-to-know-about-cat's-cradle-but-were-too-tied-up-to-ask. It's an encyclopedic gathering of string figures from all over the world with lots of interesting information about the sources of the figures and, best of all, good clear instructions and drawings that guide you in making them yourself.

Now you can amuse and amaze your friends, be the center of attention at parties, or entertain yourself endlessly, on a shoestring.

TRAVELS WITH CHARLEY

by John Steinbeck
Bantam Books, 1962

The "search for America" has become one of our national clichés. It's hard to talk about it without sounding corny. Back in the early 1960s, maybe it wasn't so trite. That's when John Steinbeck saddled up his pick-up truck and camper, named Rocinante after Don Quixote's horse, and, along with his poodle Charley, took off to drive through these here United States and find something out.

Of course we all know that the search for America is one shape the search for self takes, an attempt to chart personal geography. A good many of us harbor Steinbeck's urge to take off, to leave everything behind and travel up and down, back and forth across this country, and learn something about ourselves in the process.

Steinbeck traveled three months and thousands of miles. He met a lot of regular folks and had a few really dramatic encounters. His way was to go alone, with no preconceptions, to keep his senses and his mind open, to pay attention to things, and, finally, not to wrap things up in nice neat bundles of conclusions. America sprawls across a hefty piece of this planet; there's no way to contain it in a collection of declarative sentences.

Travels with Charley works as a piece of personal journalism. Steinbeck is an affectionate observer and reporter. The America he saw was his America. All of us would see different Americas, Americas of our own.

BEYOND SOLITAIRE

by Sid Sackson
Pantheon Books, 1976

If you're tired of solitaire but aren't up for the Sunday *Times* crossword puzzle, you might try some of Sid Sackson's games-for-one.

"Four-Color" has you color in angular shapes on a game sheet without letting two shapes of the same color touch.

"Pin Ball" simulates a pinball machine—throws of the dice determine how far and in what direction the ball moves.

"Profit and Loss" is a stock market game in which you can do a couple of years worth of trading on the Big Board and wind up a millionaire or a pauper.

"Mountains and Valleys" has you try to arrange pairs of numbers from dice throws in such a way that identical or consecutive numbers are contiguous.

"No Way" is a variation on a maze.

"Buried Treasure" is a hunt for loot on a grid.

Beyond Solitaire includes instructions for these six solitary games, game sheets, and dice cards. You supply the colored pencils. And you supply the quiet time when there's no one coming over, no place to go, no good book in reach, and nothing on TV.

HOW TO GET CONTROL OF YOUR TIME AND YOUR LIFE

by Alan Lakein
Signet Books, 1974

Too many of us seem to have too little time for the "important" things—friends, leisure, creative work. There seem to be a billion and one demands on our meager store of that precious commodity, and we give it out piecemeal, with little sense of who or what is getting it. If only we had time, we'd . . . .

Well, Alan Lakein tells us we *do* have the time, but we are inveterate fritterers. If we really want time, he says, we can get it by sorting the important from the trivial in our lives. It isn't simply a matter of getting better organized: "If you think that to 'get control' of your time and your life means becoming super-organized . . . let me assure you that is not the case," he writes. "Too much organization is as ineffective as too little." The over-organizer eats up much of his time just getting organized—"making lists, updating lists, los-

ing lists."

The key, says Lakein, is making some hard decisions about priorities—discarding superfluous activities and making a time plan to accommodate what we really want to do. This book is filled with practical advice about how to accomplish this—from scheduling to using leisure time, commuting time, waiting-for-the-bus time, even sleeping time. Those plagued by acute time shortages might benefit from time spent reading *How To Get Control of Your Time and Your Life*.

THE GREAT ESCAPE

edited by Min Yee
Bantam Books, 1974

The Great Escape is a catalogue of delights for the mind, body, and spirit. Here are 1001 ways to get away from the routine and the humdrum. Cast the I Ching, play music on a push-button telephone, turn your car into a vegetable garden, enter a sandcastle contest, backpack the coast of British Columbia, take a freighter around the world, play space war, learn Zen meditation, set a world record. This book tells you where to go, to whom to write, and what to do to get going.

Maybe none of the goodies catalogued herein will tempt you away from an overstuffed chair and a glass of brandy on a Saturday night. Still, just reading *The Great Escape* of a quiet evening can be a great escape all by itself.

Self

TO ME,
   JUST WANTED TO SAY
HOW MUCH I LIKE YOU
AND ENJOY YOUR
COMPANY. THANKS FOR
EVERYTHING.

Voices

TAKING STOCK

When I have problems I sit down and write volumes. Recently I wrote 16 pages at one sitting. It was a good catharsis. Sometimes I'll write it as a letter to somebody, but I don't mail it. One time, after an unhappy affair, I wrote down everything that happened from the beginning. After I finished writing I saw so much I had missed when I was involved in it. And I thought, "My God, why didn't you see that right from the start?"

Martha A., married 10 years,
divorced 5 years, age 37

I get to know myself better through conversations with friends in which I play things back, bounce things off them.

I also find it very profound to take acid or mescaline alone. It's a very clarifying experience. I usually go through all the emotions that I've been feeling and even those I wasn't aware I had. I replay situations from different perspectives. I don't do it with other people because I reveal so much about myself. I don't know if I can deal with being that honest with other people.

Jesse F., age 34

I keep a dream journal and a daily journal. For about a year and a half following my divorce I was feeling pretty depressed a lot of the time. It was helpful to come home and just write to get rid of that depressed feeling.

Now I also try to write whenever I'm feeling up about something. I've kept the journal for two and a half years. It's fun to go back through it and read how I felt two years ago. Things haven't changed that much. I guess I feel more stable now. But I still go up and down.

Holly H., married 3 years,
divorced 3 years, age 29

I don't keep a diary. I used to worry about my life. But I've given all that up, worrying about should I be doing something other than what I'm doing. I don't keep track of things. I don't think about that at all.

Ellen B., married 22 years,
divorced 3 years, age 58

I learn a lot by reading. That forces me to think about certain things. I am always taking stock of where I am and what I want to do. It's a continual thing.

I get very little feedback from other people, but I will talk to myself. Usually it's about business. I'm just jabbering along while driving, going over what I'm going to say to the next person.

Patrick R., married 4 years,
divorced 2 years, age 34

GROWING YOUR SELF

I push myself pretty much. I really do believe that this is the only shot you've got. This is it. It's just not worth it to be any less than everything I can be. I feel like I've been given a lot of the tools. I figure anything I want to do is possible. I ask myself, "Is there something you're not doing that you want to do? Why not? What's stopping you?"

I feel like mostly I have done it myself.

I've pushed myself through those places. And there were some hard ones. I didn't have any help at all. It was very painful. I guess I get a little bit angry when I see people who go to Esalen or one thing and another and they are trying to get all these things, but they don't want the pain.

Pamela R., age 32

I'm finding people who are interested in some of the same things I'm interested in, who want to examine some of the same issues. When I talk about my life I know it's important to my friend. I know she is listening. And the things that she says in some ways apply to me. The sharing is important. I need it because I live alone. I need to work some things out against other people who are similarly inclined and to get to that level of honesty without feeling I'm imposing on them or that they're going to be judgmental.

It's rare to find someone that I can express my vulnerabilities to. Some people, especially those in couples, are afraid of some of the things I talk about. Not just afraid. They're not able to tune into what I'm saying. Maybe it's because I've had so much time to examine my life—probably too much. It seems to me my married friends' lives take on a quality that's almost simpler without necessarily being less interesting. They don't always hang everything out to look at. I think I do, and my life is becoming increasingly more complicated that way. I'm not always sure that I'm glad this is happening, but it's almost unavoidable.

I'm not saying all single people are so introspective, but it's true for the few single people I'm getting to know really well. And so it's easier for me to talk to them than my couple friends. I really feel single people are forced to examine their lives just because of the way they live.

Donna R., married 2 years,
divorced 7 years, age 30

I don't consciously work for "personal growth." I have always liked myself. I will take a class if something interests me or do something "cultural" because I'll enjoy it, rather than to improve myself.

Ruth G., age 46

GETTING HELP

I'm reluctant to admit I need help even when I do need it. I seldom go to someone and say, "Look, I need help." What I may do is tell a friend, over a drink, what's going on in my life. I might not even say, "I want your opinion" or "Give me help." And, whether or not I get any advice or reaction, sometimes just verbalizing makes me feel better. There are two people I feel I can talk to about anything. Knowing that they're there gives me a deep-rooted feeling of security and happiness.

The other thing I'll do when I'm troubled is sleep. I remember the old line "Most fears are born out of fatigue and loneliness." I'll try to clear my head out by avoiding alcohol

and just resting. I find the passage of time itself will solve many of the problems I'm wrestling with.

George P., age 25

We were in marriage counseling and after we split up I kept going. I still go occasionally. It helps me get out what I'm angry about. I'll be in a really high space and I'll be flying along real nice. I'll be snuggling in bed with somebody and then my wife will telephone right in the middle of everything and that will spin me out. Then I'll go for some counseling.

Larry H., married 4 years,
separated 2 years, age 32

I have some people who are very good acquaintances though not good friends. I'll call up such a person and say, "Hey, do you want to do something?" I'm looking for help but I won't tell her that, not because I'd be embarrassed but simply because it would lay a burden on her. I don't know if she would handle it as well if she knew she was supposed to be helping. So I'll just say, "Let's go out to eat" and for me it provides the company that I need to take my mind off something.

Sally A., age 33

DECISIONS

I found out from the way I handled our breakup that my vision of things is top-notch. I trust my feelings. I used to confuse other people's problems with my own. I don't do that any more. I can separate other people's problems from mine. I don't worry about their troubles.

Larry H., married 4 years,
separated 2 years, age 32

I do have a certain amount of difficulty making decisions. I'm often irrational, almost passionate, in the way I make choices. Sometimes I will consult a diverse group of friends, sometimes casual acquaintances. I'll even ask people I meet in bars, on the street, on a bus. I'll say, "Hey, what do you think of this?" I am curious and concerned about what other people think and I'll consider their reactions. But, ultimately, because it's my life, I'll make the decision myself, after several days of mulling it over.

George P., age 25

I sometimes ask my mother but I pretty much know what she's going to say. She's very conservative. So I always balance her comments by going to somebody else who also would have a predictable but contrary sort of reaction. I have a tremendous need to talk and usually find during any crisis that I have to talk to about three different people before I get something resolved. I'm apologetic about that. I think I ought to be more independent. But I seem to have that need, so what the hell?

Martha A., married 10 years, divorced 5 years, age 37

A book that has been very helpful to me is *The Windows of Tarot*. I do Tarot readings all the time. They're very powerful for me. The cards represent every possible human feeling and emotion and trait—spiritual, carnal, material, love—all these things.

Jesse F., age 34

I talk over major decisions with my friends. I'm a dropper-inner to my friends who are drop-inable. I run with my problems right over to my friends. Or I'll get on the phone. I'm aware that ultimately it's my decision, but I want other people's opinions. They tell me something and I say, "Well, what about this?" And I try to argue them out of their position. My good friends are very much involved in my life and they expect all this.

Sara C., age 31

SPIRITUALITY

Religion plays a great role in my life. It always has. I've been going to church ever since I was born. I feel like something's missing if I don't take part in some kind of religious activity. The main thing is going to church on Sunday. I don't enter into the social life of the church—I need spiritual help, I don't need the social life. The church carried me through the death of my son.

Eleanor M., married 32 years, widowed 10 years, age 73

I go to church, not regularly. It's more for philosophical satisfaction than spiritual guidance. I like to hear somebody talk about the problems of life. I don't carry on a dialogue with God. He doesn't pay much attention to me, so I don't have that.

Karl C., married twice, divorced 10 years, age 68

My whole outlook is spiritual. I believe in God. I try to express my religious feeling through my art.

Mark B., age 28

Spiritual activity just boils down to working on yourself.

Ellen B., married 22 years, divorced 3 years, age 58

Every now and then, at a holiday or when I have a certain need, I'll walk into a place of worship no matter what kind it is, just sit down or kneel down for a minute, say a silent prayer, and leave. I have very little patience for traditional services.

George P., age 25

GROWING OLD

I'm not worried much about it now. I guess I've been influenced by Babba Ram Dass' *Be Here Now*. Here I am right now. There's really

no past and really no future. Everything that's happening to me in my life is happening now. It's not worth thinking about what's going to happen in 15 years. That's just an eternity away. I've got better things to worry about right now.

Bruce F., married 10 years, separated 2 years, age 38

I think about it. It's something that is rather frightening. Ideally, I would like to self-

destruct when I'm about 65. That's my date now. But it may change when one gets nearer to the point.

Lynn H., age 45

I'm not afraid of growing old alone because I am part of a Zen community. Most of my friends in it are younger than I am. I'm going to outdie them, die before they die. And this community will hold up pretty well. It's like a second family. I rent out rooms from my house to some of the Zen people, too.

Another possibility is for me to go into a retirement home. I've been thinking a little bit about that. My mother is in a retirement home. She likes it very much. I'm very sociable. I'll probably get to the point where I'd like to play bridge every afternoon.

Ellen B., married 22 years,
divorced 3 years, age 58

I chose this retirement community partly so I wouldn't grow old alone. There are three hundred people that live here.

Eleanor M., married 32 years,
widowed 10 years, age 73

I don't have to worry about that because the relationships that I have now are very rich. And I've purposefully done that. I've made commitments with a lot of people. I trust them and they trust me. These people will be in my life forever.

Larry H., married 4 years,
separated 2 years, age 32

HEALTH

It would be nice to have someone around when I'm sick. I'm sick in bed only very rarely, but when it happens I always think of my mother. She's been dead for ten years.

Lynn H., age 45

I like being sick. Being sick is a very pleasant thing because you can lie in bed all day and read and nobody can see you not being able to breathe. I just let my body go through it. It doesn't scare me. I take my medicine and go to bed.

Cindy W., age 24

Being sick is something I've always been afraid of. Once I was in bed with a fever of about 104°. I had fantasies that someday someone would come and discover my decomposing body. There have been times when nobody has checked up on me for days or weeks.

Jesse F., age 34

Song of Myself

WALT WHITMAN

1

I celebrate myself, and sing myself,
And what I assume you shall assume,
For every atom belonging to me as good
    belongs to you.
I loafe and invite my soul,
I lean and loafe at my ease observing a
    spear of summer grass.

My tongue, every atom of my blood,
    form'd from this soil, this air,
Born here of parents born here from par-
    ents the same, and their parents the
    same,
I, now thirty-seven years old in perfect
    health begin,
Hoping to cease not till death.

Creeds and schools in abeyance,
Retiring back a while sufficed at what
    they are, but never forgotten,
I harbor for good or bad, I permit to
    speak at every hazard,
Nature without check with original
    energy.

2

Houses and rooms are full of perfumes,
    the shelves are crowded with per-
    fumes,
I breathe the fragrance myself and know
    it and like it,
The distillation would intoxicate me
    also, but I shall not let it,

The atmosphere is not a perfume, it has
no taste of the distillation, it is odor-
    less,
It is for my mouth forever, I am in love
    with it,
I will go to the bank by the wood and
    become undisguised and naked,
I am mad for it to be in contact with me.

The smoke of my own breath,
Echoes, ripples, buzz'd whispers, love-
    root, silk-thread, crotch and vine,
My respiration and inspiration, the beat-
    ing of my heart, the passing of blood
    and air through my lungs,
The sniff of green leaves and dry leaves,
    and of the shore and dark-color'd
    sea-rocks, and of hay in the barn,
The sound of the belch'd words of my
    voice loos'd to the eddies of the
    wind,
A few light kisses, a few embraces, a
    reaching around of arms,
The play of shine and shade on the trees
    as the supple boughs wag,
The delight alone or in the rush of the
    streets, or along the fields and hill-
    sides,
The feeling of health, the full-noon trill,
    the song of me rising from bed and
    meeting the sun.

Have you reckon'd a thousand acres
    much? have you reckon'd the earth
    much?
Have you practis'd so long to learn to
    read?

Have you felt so proud to get at the meaning of poems?

Stop this day and night with me and you shall possess the origin of all poems,
You shall possess the good of the earth and sun,(there are millions of suns left,)
You shall no longer take things at second or third hand, nor look through the eyes of the dead, nor feed on the spectres in books,
You shall not look through my eyes either, nor take things from me,
You shall listen to all sides and filter them from your self.

3

I have heard what the talkers were talking, the talk of the beginning and the end,
But I do not talk of the beginning or the end.

There was never any more inception than there is now,
Nor any more youth or age than there is now,
And will never be any more perfection than there is now,
Nor any more heaven or hell than there is now.

Urge and urge and urge,
Always the procreant urge of the world.

Out of the dimness opposite equals advance, always substance and increase, always sex,
Always a knit of identity, always distinction, always a breed of life.

To elaborate is no avail, learn'd and unlearn'd feel that it is so.

Sure as the most certain sure, plumb in the uprights, well entretied, braced in the beams,
Stout as a horse, affectionate, haughty, electrical,
I and this mystery here we stand.

Clear and sweet is my soul, and clear and sweet is all that is not my soul.
Lack one lacks both, and the unseen is proved by the seen,
Till that becomes unseen and receives proof in its turn.

Showing the best and dividing it from the worst age vexes age,
Knowing the perfect fitness and equanimity of things, while they discuss I am silent, and go bathe and admire myself.

From *Leaves of Grass* by Walt Whitman

Books

TELLING YOUR STORY

by Sam Keene and Anne Fox
Signet Books, 1973

Man is a story-telling animal, the authors tell us. It is stories—myths, legends, biographies—that connect us with the past and the future, that speak to us in the most intimate and immediate sense of who we are and where we fit in the scheme of things.

For a variety of reasons, Keene and Fox write, we've lost awareness of storytelling as a way to dramatize and order human existence. *Telling Your Story* aims to help reestablish personal storytelling as a central process in our lives.

So how do we tell stories? What do we tell stories about? The exercises in this book help on both counts. Many ask questions the answers to which are story-making material. They suggest making lists you can use in your story: "Make a list of ten words or phrases that describe you best." They provide examples for every kind of story they suggest.

Whether or not you take the exercises to heart as composition assignments and follow through by making your own stories, just giving them some thought ought to help you gain a broader and deeper view of yourself.

BITTERSWEET: SURVIVING AND GROWING FROM LONELINESS

by Terri Schultz
Thomas Y. Crowell Co., 1976

This book is a kind of gentle journey through the various provinces of loneliness. Terri Schultz asks us to see loneliness not simply as a negative experience but also as one of the central, necessary experiences of human life, and as possibility.

Many of us are inclined to treat our episodes of loneliness the way children treat vegetables—by grimacing and hurrying through them as fast as we can. Sometimes that hurrying means a headlong dive into some really unsatisfactory situations and relationships. For instance, there seem to be any number of people who get themselves stuck in bad marriages because they've decided anything is better than that awful loneliness.

Schultz pleads for a less horrified response to loneliness, for using times of loneliness to pay attention to some deeper parts of ourselves, for exercising restraint when we are inclined to accept just about anything as a substitute for loneliness. She examines the ways people use their loneliness to help themselves or to hurt themselves. She discusses sex as a sometime cure for and as an aggravation of loneliness. She writes about the importance of friends and the joys and difficulties they bring.

Bittersweet is basically a personal book, an experience of the tones and textures of loneliness.

AT A JOURNAL WORKSHOP

by Ira Progoff
Dialogue House Library, 1975

The "Intensive Journal" is a technique for self-help, self-discovery, personal growth that is remarkable in its essential simplicity and its obviousness. It is, at its very heart, a diary, a personal book of days. But Ira Progoff has taken the diary form and stretched and stretched and stretched it so it includes so much more than accounts of what happened when. The "Intensive Journal" is, in fact, a

THE INTENSIVE JOURNAL

The *Intensive Journal* is specifically designed to provide an instrument and techniques by which persons can discover within themselves the resources they did not know they possessed. It is to enable them to draw the power of deep contact out of the actual experiences of their lives so that they can recognize their own identity and harmonize it with the larger identity of the universe as they experience it. Where they had negated themselves, they can by means of their *Intensive Journal* work, give their lives full value.

The specific means of achieving this contact with the inner resources of one's life is by the regular and disciplined use of the *Intensive Journal* with its progressive exercises. The effective principle operating in this is that, when a person is shown how to reconnect himself with the contents and the continuity of his life, the inner thread of movement by which his life has been unfolding reveals itself to him by itself. Given the opportunity, a life crystallizes out of its own nature, revealing its meaning and its goal. This is the self-integrating principle of life which the Journal procedures make available to us as persons.

As an individual works in the Journal Feedback process, the past experiences of his life gradually fit into place, times of exaltation and times of despair, moments of hope and anger, cries and crossroads, partial failures and successes. As we use them over a period of time, the procedures of the *Intensive Journal* make it possible for all the events and relationships of our life to show us what they were *for*, what their purpose was in our lives, and what they wish to tell us for our future. Thus we gradually discover that our life has been going somewhere, however blind we have been to its direction and however unhelpful to it we ourselves may have been. We find that a connective thread has been forming beneath the surface of our lives, carrying the meaning that has been trying to establish itself in our existence. It is the inner continuity of our lives. As we recognize and identify ourselves with it, we see the inner myth that has been guiding our lives unknown to ourselves.

In the course of the gradual and cumulative work by which an individual recognizes the nonconscious guidance that has been directing his personal life involvements, he perceives that the peaks and the valleys are of equal importance. Fron one point of view, all are necessary, for the high is not possible without the low. In a more fundamental sense, however, he recognizes that the essence lies not in the events of his life in themselves, not in the things that have happened to him, but in his inner relationship to those events. At the moment when they were actually taking place, his relation to those events may have been inadequate because of many small fears and limited understanding. For that, he may feel guilty, angry, and negative toward himself. As the larger perspective opens through the Journal work, however, a new quality of relationship can be established to the events of the past. The continuity of our life renews itself, and we have a fresh opportunity.

From *At A Journal Workshop*

medium for growth. And it can so shape itself to each individual, it so readily can become a deep and personal mode of self-examination/self-expression that it really doesn't feel like a gimmick or device at all.

At a Journal Workshop presents the "Intensive Journal" system that Progoff has developed over a period of years. He says at the outset that the system "plays an active role in reconstructing a life, but it does so without imposing any external categories or interpretations . . . it remains neutral and open-ended so as to maintain the integrity of each person's development . . . ."

Among the components of the "Intensive Journal" are: a Period Log, which records the present texture of "Where I Am Now in My Life"; a Twilight Imagery Log, a recording of unbidden images that occur in a kind of semiconscious state between sleeping and waking; the Daily Log, much like a diary; Steppingstones, a record of significant movement and change; the Life History Log, which records all the facts of the individual's past; Journal Feedback, which includes "dialogues" with various people and aspects of one's life.

Progoff leads the reader very carefully through all parts of the entire "Intensive Journal" process. His ideas are exciting, his explanations are clear, his sensibility is humane.

SELF ANALYSIS

by Karen Horney
W.W. Norton & Company, Inc., 1942

In this classic of psychological literature, Karen Horney presents the compelling and convincing argument that ordinary people, not trained as psychiatrists, psychologists, or psychoanalysts, are able successfully to analyze themselves.

Horney doesn't propose some quicky pop gimmick but rather an approach firmly grounded in the psychoanalytic methods of Freud and his followers, relying chiefly on careful observation, free association, and dream analysis.

The fundamental goal of analysis has always been to discover the unconscious motivations that cause us to act the way we do. Those motivations may result in physical difficulties, neurotic behavior, or, less severely, in impediments to continued personal growth and fulfillment. Once we expose those motivations we are usually able to get rid of the physical disorder, stop the pathological behavior, live and grow in richer, more positive ways.

Self Analysis includes a clear and thorough explanation of the psychoanalytic approach, an ample discussion of the possibilities and limitations of self-analysis, a careful presentation of the systematic use of this technique, and a lengthy example of the self-analysis done by a woman trying to rid herself of a morbid dependency on a man.

Without being simplistic, Horney makes many of the intricacies of analysis easily understandable to the lay person. Her writing is warm and human. And her thesis that we might help ourselves in some really profound ways is certainly encouraging.

GROWING OLDER

by Margaret Hellie Huyck
Spectrum Books, 1974

Growing old alone is a strong concern of many single people. In general, however, the problems of older people have only recently become a subject of interest in our society. Youth-oriented as we are, we have systematically failed to pay attention to that increasingly large segment of our population over 50 years old. *Growing Older* is a kind of primer on aging, a collection of essays that considers everything from senior-citizen sex to the advent of death.

The book looks with care and compassion on the problems as well as the possibilities of old age. It is true that the body slows down and gets a little creaky. It is true that 65-year-olds can't perform sexually as often as 25-year-olds. It is also true that vigorous activity doesn't need to stop simply because of age. The book steers clear of sentimentality, but not tenderness. Margaret Mead writes a lovely essay on being a grandmother. Clark Moustakas tells a moving story of a lonely old man who finally penetrated his loneliness and came out on the other side filled with life and strength.

Like death, aging is an ingredient in our lives. Like death, it won't go away. We may never be able to prepare ourselves fully for all that aging and death bring. But neither do we have to acquiesce to the myths that seek to convince us that life ends at 60. The tough minds that fight against those debilitating fictions live vigorously, however long they survive.

We need to ponder aging; we need to know the truth about it. *Growing Older* might help us understand more.

SIDDHARTHA

by Hermann Hesse
Bantam Books, 1951

Siddhartha is a classic tale of the search for wisdom and peace. Siddhartha is a young, wealthy Brahmin who grows dissatisfied with his life and develops a powerful longing to experience the "Absolute Truth" of life. With his friend Govinda he leaves his comfortable life and becomes an ascetic living in the wilds. Through various ascetic practices and disciplines he develops many spiritual powers but fails to "lose" himself completely.

Siddhartha and Govinda leave their ascetic practices and go to hear the Buddha teach. Govinda chooses to become a disciple of the Buddha; Siddhartha's restless mind won't let him remain. He decides he must learn about the world, in particular about the world of love and desire, so he becomes the "student" of a beautiful courtesan. In order to be with her he must have money, so he sets about becoming a wealthy merchant. For many years he lives the worldly life of a rich man, but finally finds he is disgusted with it and flees, leaving it all behind much as he did when he was a young man leaving his family home. He at last finds the peace he has always sought on the banks of a river. Alone, with only the sounds of the river, he learns to give up his restless seeking and discover the truth that was always there.

The search for "meaning" or "peace" or whatever we may wish to call it is essentially a solitary one. Siddhartha, sitting alone, listening to the river, illuminates that search.

PASSAGES: PREDICTABLE CRISES OF ADULT LIFE

by Gail Sheehy
E.P. Dutton & Co., Inc., 1976

Only recently have psychologists begun to study developmental stages in adults. Far from being a reliefless plateau or a long, slow slide into old age, adulthood is as rich with changes and crises as childhood or adolescence.

Ages 22-29 Sheehy calls "Provisional Adulthood." This is a time for weaning from parents, for experimenting with adult roles, for exploring work, for shaping "a vision of oneself in the world."

Ages 29-32 make up the "Age Thirty Transition." One common pattern in this stage is the tearing up of the life one spent most of one's twenties putting together. It may mean striking out on a secondary road toward a new vision, or converting a dream of running for President into a more realistic goal.

Ages 32-39 are a time of hard work, great creative/productive energy. There is a need to become fully independent, to call one's own shots.

Ages 39-43 compose the "Mid-Life Transition," a painfully difficult time when the first twinges of mortality begin to be felt.

Ages 43-50 Sheehy calls "Restabilization and Flowering." Once the mid-life crisis has been passed through, a new, mellower person emerges, more realistic, less threatened.

The message that clearly emerges from *Passages* is that whatever outward shape the stages take—Sheehy's examples are for the most part people whose lives fit into conventional middle-class configurations—all of us have rather insistent inner clocks ticking off growth and change from the minute we're born until the minute we die.

Single Again

Voices

THE EX-MATE

She still wants me to contact her if I feel like it. Do I find room for her or do I put myself in a little box and shut her out completely for the rest of my life—and create more pain? I want to reach the point where I'm not treating every contact with her as a crisis. I want to be able to get a letter from her without getting angry or without thinking it's the biggest thing that ever happened to me.

Larry H., married 4 years,
separated 2 years, age 32

We see each other as much as we can, given that we live in different parts of the country. I feel good about that. In fact, I read an article for psychiatrists that said it was a good idea to support someone who is still seeing an ex-mate. I think it is important not to see a former partner in the period immediately following the split because that makes it difficult to cut the tie. But later on is different. There is something we have to share. I don't have any expectations but I feel very close to him and I can enjoy that.

Donna R., married 2 years,
divorced 7 years, age 30

We have never had a fight. We have kept the peace mainly because I have kept the peace. Because of a business failure he was going to commit suicide, so I lent him money. I have not taken him to court for non-child-support even after he got a good job. I have knocked myself out keeping the peace for the sake of my child and also because I feel that the

wear and tear on many divorced women of getting their due ruins them. I don't know. I feel I can grow old more gracefully if I don't get mad and don't fight. It's easier for me to make it without any support from him and to keep the peace. So we have a joking, friendly relationship. It's aggravating for me, but I keep up a good act.

Jennifer F., married 5 years,
divorced 5 years, age 34

He's married now. And we're still friends. He calls me maybe once a month. Maybe we'll go out to lunch. I don't think his wife likes it but I think that's their problem. She can't understand why we're friends still. I figure it's O.K. if we're having lunch. I don't see why we should stop being friends because she's jealous.

Holly H., married 3 years,
divorced 3 years, age 29

THE TRANSITION

My roommate, I think, was the biggest help. He was going through the same things I was and we were able to listen to each other and get out a lot of our pain and anger and fear.

Norman S., married 6 years,
divorced 3 years, age 33

You have to really keep your network of friends. You have to have very sustaining, nurturing relationships. I have gone out of my way to maintain that. Before I split up I used to rely on my love relationship for all my nurturing. Nurturing was all tied up

with sex. But now I'm trying to change that. I'm trying to get support from my friends. The trouble is, my single friends are always going out on dates. And my married friends don't go out at all. So it's hard to find people.

I've talked with my friends about how they've handled moving from a couple situation back to being single again. I tell them I'm depressed and they say, "Well, it's O.K. to be depressed because you really have lost a lot and you have to make all these adjustments. So, if you're depressed, don't think

any less of yourself because that's the way it goes." I have a very good friend who went through it a while before me. I spend a lot of time talking with her. I can see what a full, rich life she has now, and that helps. But it took her a while too.

Also, I wrote a song about what happened in my relationship. It was the first song I ever wrote. But it made it radiantly clear to me that we were finished. Whenever I start getting sentimental about her, I play that song and I remember what I have gone through and that helps me be less sentimental about it.

Jesse F., age 34

For the first couple of weeks I was in a daze. But as with most problems, whether they are business or not, I took a lot of long walks and just really worked it out in my own head. I can't exactly say at what point it was, but finally I just said, "That's it. It's over and now I'm into something else." It happened pretty quick.

I basically worked it out myself. I talked to a few people but nobody really close. I guess the most helpful person was my mother. She seemed to be the one who understood me best and could listen and ask the right questions.

*Patrick R., married 4 years,
divorced 2 years, age 34*

I collapsed. I felt terrible. I just felt lousy for quite a long time. I tried to carry on my life pretty much the same. And I got a great deal of help from my friends, just talking to them. They helped me feel that I was O.K.

Once in a while I'd drink a lot. Two or three times, I think. Then I did something better than drinking. I got a boy friend and that helped me forget about my ex-husband immediately. I was fine when I was with this new man. I didn't remember Ted at all. But when the boy friend wasn't around, then I would think about my former husband. All in all, it helps a lot to have someone new. If you're rejected it certainly makes you feel better to have somebody come along and say they think you're pretty great.

*Ellen B., married 22 years,
divorced 3 years, age 58*

The hardest thing was the stigma of not being able to make my marriage work. I was more concerned about how other people would see that. I wasn't too sure whether it was better to say I had never been married or to say I was divorced. I really had no concept of what a single woman who was approaching her mid-20s was supposed to be like.

Now, of course, I'm not embarrassed at all. Times have changed. And I'm living in a community where being divorced and being single is common. I think I would be a little scared moving to some place where I would feel isolated. Because even here, being single still has its moments of feeling like the odd person out. Deep inside me I still sense that it's a couple society. Often, when I try something new for myself, doing something I usually associate with couples—like eating out in a restaurant at night—I don't go into it with a great deal of enthusiasm. I don't expect it to be easy or even positive. I'm often surprised that it's as good as it is. And I also feel defensive about it when I share my experience with others. It's hard to tell whether it's a problem in me or whether it's the society that makes me feel defensive and different and, in subtle ways, a little freakish.

*Donna R., married 2 years,
divorced 7 years, age 30*

The divorce hit me hard. I was scared economically because so many men default on support payments, though, as it turned out, my ex-husband has been very dependable.

I was also afraid of the loneliness and I didn't like the idea of being a single parent. All of that depressed me and I used to sit on the back porch and drink beer and gaze off into space and cry. I just wallowed in it and let myself go completely. I was wishing for insanity. I thought that that would be a nice out. But, unfortunately, I remained sane and had to deal with it all.

*Martha A., married 10 years,
divorced 5 years, age 37*

I came home from work one day and my wife said, "I've got a secret. I want you to guess it." And I said, "Well, the only thing you would keep secret from me is that you've been to bed with somebody else." She said, "How did you guess?"

So I spent a few nights crying and being real confused and thinking about suicide. She said it was wonderful that she had decided to open up our marriage and that she thought it was no problem since I had already accepted everything else that she had done and had always encouraged her in anything that she thought was her own growth. Why should this be any different?

I said, "Well, hell, this is different." And I split.

I started trying to figure out what was going on, whether I was crazy or whether everybody else was crazy. After about three or four months of just coming home and crashing, I started going to bookstores at night. I read everything from consciousness-raising materials to psychoanalytic theory to existential philosophy. I wanted insight into what was going on in me. I wanted to know whether what I was feeling was healthy or not. I just sat on the floor at the bookstore pulling books off the shelves and going through them one after another. I learned a lot that helped get me together.

Larry H., married 4 years,
separated 2 years, age 32

My husband wouldn't admit that he was dying when he was. And it didn't help me much because he didn't plan with me what would happen later. I had to do much of the planning after his death. I was amply insured. But we never openly discussed the matter of death.

I had to deal with selling our big house and other matters pretty much by myself. I've always been able to handle my emotions, though—I've never been a crybaby. I didn't let out my feelings when he died. My doctor was so upset because I couldn't cry. I just couldn't. He said, "You can have a nervous breakdown holding your emotions in." I just couldn't let go. Besides, I was so busy. I was involved in my work and in many other things. I was just trying to make my life go on the way it had always been going.

Of course there were changes. But my friends were marvelous to me, couples that we knew intimately. They added me to their guest lists just like they always had before. But I was not so dumb not to know that that would soon come to an end. People don't continue treating you as a couple when you're not a couple any more. For a while they take good care of you, but it won't last forever. Before it stopped in my case I took a long trip, sold my house, and moved to another town where I knew people whom, I felt, I could relate to as a single person.

I didn't really have models for how to be a successful widow. I just had models of what I wasn't going to be like. You know, people complaining all the time about the loss of their husbands. My mother was like that. She never did get over my father's death. She spent so much time talking about him that she made herself miserable. You should, I think, talk about your troubles. That's the only healthy thing to do. But not to too great an extent. I wasn't going to be like that.

Eleanor M., married 32 years,
widowed 10 years, age 73

Leaving Home

CONSTANCE BERESFORD-HOWE

The real surprise—to me anyway—was not really what I did, but how I felt afterwards. Shocked, of course. But not guilty. You might say, and be right, that the very least a woman can be is shocked when she walks out on a sick and blameless husband after forty years. But to feel no guilt at all—feel nothing, in fact, but simple relief and pleasure—that did seem odd, to say the least. How annoying for God (not to mention Adam), after all, if Eve had just walked out of Eden without waiting to be evicted, and left behind her pangs of guilt, as it were, with her leaf apron.

In any case, I just walked out. There was no quarrel with Burt. No crisis at all. The clock chimed nine-thirty. I laid down the breakfast tray carefully (an apple and a cup of cocoa) on the hall desk, and went to my room and packed. Not a word to anyone, even myself, by way of apology or excuse. Why? And why just then? Truly I'm not sure yet, although my name is Eva.

And who would believe it possible to wake up in these circumstances as happy as a birthday child? I opened my eyes into a perfect, self-centered bliss without past or future, and rejoiced in everything I saw. Inspected every inch of my new place without a twinge of dismay, and then sat down to count my money—or what was left of it. Even this didn't depress me. . . .

I set up my books on an end-table, plugged in my radio, and switched it on. Mozart obliged. I found an old peanut-butter jar and drank rather a lot of sherry out of it. When dusk painted the windows an opaque blue I heated soup and ate it, then scrubbed out the bath, filled it up, and had a long, contented soak with *Playboy*. After that I brushed my teeth and climbed into bed. Clean, happy, and innocent as a lamb. For a few hours I slept fathoms deep in the dark, without a dream.

And then I woke up to hear my heart beating. I began then to count and think. Great mistakes, both.

The trouble is, you never can escape a righteous upbringing. Right now I was a success—an escaped prisoner never likely to be recaptured. What's more, I hadn't the slightest urge to explain or apologize to Burt or Neil. And yet, I wanted to justify my ways to somebody—God, perhaps—because, come to think of it, nobody else really knew me. A bit of cheek, perhaps, to address Him person-to-person; if only I could write Him a letter.

Reverend Sir:
   I realize I owe You some kind of explanation for yesterday, during which I broke quite a few of Your ten rules (though I've often wondered whether Moses didn't forge some of them).
   You see, I'd just like to make it clear that I ran away not just from the servitude of nursing Burt, running the house, shopping and cleaning up, and all that drab routine. Nor from the confinement, even, though that was bad. As You know, he was haunted by the fear of fire, and hated being left alone in the house even for short intervals while I did necessary errands in the neighbourhood. He couldn't get out in the winter months himself at all, and of course it was hard for him, caged up inside his pain, to keep a sense of proportion. But one of my few pleasures, especially in the years after Neil's marriage, was browsing through antique shops, where I discovered treasures like my spinet desk, a Lismer drawing, and a Bel-

The chief duty of females, we were taught, was to practice the restraints of civilization, not explore its possibilities.

leek tea-set—all such bargains even Burt couldn't complain much. But in the last few years, he made such a misery every time I wanted to go out for a few hours on these hunts that finally I had to give them up altogether. And because that one little private pleasure was cut off, I festered with resentment. Inwardly only—though I don't claim that as a virtue; I couldn't face quarrelling.

"Burt, someone can come in and sit with you for a few hours—Janet next door has offered to, more than once."

"I don't want to be under an obligation to the neighbours."

"Well, then, why can't we pay someone to—"

"You want a stranger in here?—"

You see. It was no use reasoning with him. No use exploding in anger, either. So I said nothing; just festered. And took to eating for consolation and pleasure. Gradually I swelled with fat, loose, heavy flesh like another prison I still lug around. The doctor warned me, and prescribed pills for hypertension; it was no use. I went on eating and eating—during the day, like an addict, I bridged meals with chocolates; I ate hot rolls with butter and jam, slices of pie with whipped cream; at night I took butter tarts or a wedge of iced cake to eat in bed with a book.

After a while I came to feel as if all this fat were a sort of disguise. No one knew me. Burt, who saw me every day, least of all. Neil, who rarely saw me, had cares of his own, including four children, so he had to avoid recognizing what he knew of me. And there was no one else.

Do You realize, I wonder, what submerged identities women like me can have? How repressed and suppressed we are by a life that can give us no kind of self-expression? Unless You really are female after all, as the Women's Lib girls insist, even You can't know what it's like to be invisible for years on end. To live locked up. Never spontaneous. Never independent. Never free, even to use those four-letter words we all know, because the chief duty of females, we were taught, was to practise the restraints of civilization, not explore its possibilities.

So my solitary confinement has been pretty hard to distinguish from death itself. Oh, hell—if You'll pardon the expression—that sounds emotional and exaggerated, but You know what I mean. God, I hate whiners, and even to You I won't snivel with self-pity.

It would have been different if my life before Burt got arthritis had been full of colour and interest and the richness of love and loving. But if You don't mind my saying so, I got a damn small share of those things, so small that coming up to my seventieth year I couldn't help feeling both cheated and panicky.

Well, that's my case. Does it make any sense to You? I hope so, because, Sir, I'd like You to respect me, even if You disapprove. And I'd be glad if You could give a bit of advice on what to do with my freedom, now I've stolen it. Hoping to hear from You in the near future,

I remain,
Yours disobediently,
Eva.

Which would be all very well if God ever answered His mail.

From *The Book of Eve* by Constance Beresford-Howe

Books

LETTERS OF ALICE B. TOKLAS: STAYING ON ALONE

edited by Edward Burns
Vintage Books, 1973

Surely one of the most famous relationships in the literary world was the one between Gertrude Stein and Alice B. Toklas. The two lived together nearly 40 years, Alice taking care of all the details of their home life, creating space for Gertrude to write. From all accounts the relationship between the two was perfectly balanced between what each could give and what each needed.

Gertrude Stein died in 1946. Alice B. Toklas lived another 23 years, until she was nearly 90. *Staying On Alone* is a collection of the many, many letters she wrote during those years without her dear partner.

There are letters to publishers, friends, editors, universities, Stein devotees. Much of the correspondence is filled with Stein's presence—business doings related to the publishing of her works, reminiscences about their time together, expressions of loss and sadness and longing. But whatever the ostensible subjects, the letters are really about Toklas herself; they reveal the kind of person she was. Her years without Stein were not a decline into a bitter and regretful old age. She felt her beloved friend's absence, to be sure, but hers was such a lively spirit, such a vivacious intellect, that her time alone was the continuation of a rich and interesting life.

Besides being a document replete with literary and cultural history, *Staying On Alone* presents a marvelous example of the quality of mind and spirit that can make life alone full and rich.

BETWEEN MARRIAGE AND DIVORCE

by Susan Braudy
New American Library, 1975

Seldom do things that are really important in our personal lives happen fast; few transitions are abrupt. We often speak of "going through" something like separation or divorce as if they were long half-lit corridors that lead who-knows-where. Susan Braudy stepped into one of those corridors with an act of infidelity—after five years of an "ideal" marriage. *Between Marriage and Divorce* is a journal of the year she spent finding her way in that dim place.

Braudy's affair didn't cause her to pack up and leave her husband. It didn't even convince her that she didn't love her husband, or that she had a bad marriage. It did set in motion, or bring into consciousness, a gradual, growing awareness of herself, her aims, her needs, and her relationship with her husband. That process of awareness was not a beeline from point A to point B, but a low, often confusing, and apparently aimless wandering among all the parts of her life—family, the past, work, friends, ideals, emotions, goals.

We root for Braudy to reach a final resolution. It became clear that her marriage wasn't good for her or her husband, yet she clung to it. She didn't work to change it; she wouldn't leave. In some ways she loved Paul; the thought of his loving another woman filled her with anxieties. Ironically, the end finally came when he admitted being in love with another woman and having an affair with her.

For all those who have been there—between marriage and divorce—this book will be painfully familiar.

SURVIVAL GUIDE FOR THE SUDDENLY SINGLE

by Barbara Benson and Ben Bova
St. Martin's Press, Inc., 1974

If you're fresh out of marriage, this is your book. The format is "His" and "Hers." Barbara Benson, divorced after 15 years of marriage, writes about the problems of newly single women. Ben Bova, also divorced after 15 years of marriage (not from Barbara Benson, but wouldn't *that* have been an interesting book?), writes about the difficulties newly single men face. The authors cover such subjects as the initial adjustment, sex, children, money, friends, relatives, alternating the female and male points of view.

Survival Guide for the Suddenly Single isn't a minutely detailed guide through all the technical difficulties of the newly separated, but a sort of grab-you-by-the-lapels-and-shape-you-up series of exhortations to toughen up and get on with it. Between them, Benson and Bova have lived through most of the anxieties and seemingly insurmountable difficulties of the divorced—alimony/child support, custody of children, setting up a new home, reactions of friends and relatives, dating again—and seem to have made it in relatively good shape. Their book aims to pass on their message that the problems are manageable, that there is a life after divorce.

LEARNING TO LIVE OFF THE LAND

That first night alone, precisely at midnight, I became painfully aware that there was no toilet paper in my new apartment.

Who worried about trivialities like toilet paper? That's one of the things your wife gets when she goes shopping, right? Fine. Except now there was no wife around. After years of trying to make an unhappy marriage work, we had split.

So there I was in a darkened studio apartment, with all the stores closed, myself on the john, and no toilet paper. In fact, there wasn't much paper of any sort in the place. *Scientific American*? Sacrilege! Besides, I hadn't finished reading it yet, and the paper was too slick. The shopping bags from the evening's journey to the supermarket? (You walked right past the goddamned paper goods aisle, genius.) The newspaper?

It had been a fairly traumatic evening, this first one on my own. I had carefully bought plenty of food at the supermarket—enough canned goods to see me through a winter's siege. Of course, I had forgotten to include a can opener in my purchases. So dinner had consisted of a bologna sandwich and a bottle of Seven Up (screwtop bottle).

I finally decided on the newspaper. Classified ad section. After all, what did I need the classifieds for? I had a job, a new apartment, furniture and plenty of canned goods.

What I didn't have anymore was a wife, a family, a comfortable home well stocked with the amenities of life, such as can openers and a TV set.

It had taken me three months to actually make the split. Three months of hunting for an apartment, getting furniture and wondering if I was really doing the right thing.

From Survival Guide for the Suddenly Single

COPING:
A SURVIVAL MANUAL
FOR WOMEN ALONE

by Martha Yates
Prentice-Hall, Inc., 1976

There's hardly an issue relating to the lives of single women—particularly divorced and widowed women—that Martha Yates hasn't touched upon in this book. She addresses the nuts-and-bolts financial and legal matters as well as the emotional and psychological ones.

Young single women today may have less need of this book than their older counterparts. So much "helplessness" is merely a result of social expectations—a woman was helpless because she was expected to be, in effect, told to be, by society. And whether or not they are expert in financial and legal matters, women who face them without that artificial helplessness can certainly do as well as men in negotiating their complexities.

Women who use Yates' book are likely to get a good dose of confidence from it. Included are most, if not all, the questions a woman should ask about such matters as money, law, work, care, home repairs, travel, health, taxes, and many of the answers. In some places *Coping* is detailed and specific, in others much more general. The real point of the book is not to be a manual for solving every problem that arises, but to enlarge women's consciousness to include matters they might never have had to deal with when their mates were still around.

SUMMER BEFORE THE DARK

by Doris Lessing
Alfred A. Knopf, Inc., 1973

No writer has given more eloquent voice to the self alone than has Doris Lessing. Lessing's protagonists embody the urge for self-knowledge, an urge that sometimes seems in them as dark and primordial as the shark's instinct for blood.

In *Summer Before the Dark*, Kate Brown, a handsome, 45-year-old middle-class British mother and housewife, is left alone for a summer by her doctor husband, off to

America, and her grown children, off on various trips. Kate takes a job and begins to see herself in a new way, temporarily stripped of family and old roles. That new perception is just the beginning. Through dreams and reflections and introspection so intense that sometimes the reader may feel the need to put down the book to rest from it, Kate cuts away layer after layer of herself, getting ever closer to the bone.

It's the bone that is the real self. Those other Kates were merely projections that she stepped into, one after another, all her life, taking refuge in them, taking some comfort. And though they were just images, mirages, they fused with her, became in some way a real part of her, and the process of peeling them away is agonizing.

Kate's summer alone changes her enormously. She discards much of what she was. Yet Lessing doesn't do any tidying up or any moralizing about all this. She doesn't promise that there is any "reward" for self-knowledge. There is no sense that Kate will now lead a "happy" or "richer" life because of what she has gone through, no sense that she has changed for the "better," just a sense that she has changed, that some very old, inexorable force is at work in her, moving her into ever deeper and darker regions of the self.

WIDOW

by Lynn Caine
Bantam Books, 1974

We might approach a book like this somewhat tentatively, expecting long, gushy passages of sentimentalism and self-pity. But there's none of that in *Widow*. Lynn Caine doesn't trivialize the death of her husband or her own true and deep grief by indulging in superficial philosophizing. She simply tells her story in a spare and direct way.

First there is the year of her husband's dying. She does not pretend to be dignified and brave, although "In the back of my mind all the time was the magnificent Jacqueline Kennedy in her widow's weeds, holding a child by either hand." She is frank about her anger, her frustration, her confusion: "I didn't cherish my children. I hated them. I hated those kids. Hated them! They were too much. When Martin was gone, how would I take care of them?" And as her husband wastes away, she reflects on her sexuality: "No man stirred my passions . . . yet I wanted men to see me as a woman." While away from home on a business trip she has a brief, "tawdry" sexual encounter with a stranger.

After her husband's death, Caine wanders from anger to numbness to a special kind of "craziness." It is no easy trip, but a wrenching journey through a landscape of anguish. Finally, she makes it through all the pain and loneliness and reappears a strong and new woman. One reviewer put it well by saying that *Widow* "may well turn out to be *the* textbook on how to cope with loneliness."

AS SPRING FOLLOWS WINTER

"I know of only one functional psychiatric disorder whose cause is known, whose features are distinctive and whose course is usually predictable. And that is grief, the reaction to loss," says Dr. Colin Murray Parkes, an eminent British psychiatrist and a member of the Tavistock Institute in London. And yet this "disorder," he complains, is not even touched on in "most of the best known general textbooks of psychiatry."

Unbelievable? Not really. I can understand why death and grief are so neglected, even by the professionals. Death is the last taboo in our society. We are terrified of it, much as the aborigines were terrified of an eclipse. And with far less reason. After all, dying is the ultimate human task. Although it is the end of life, it is part of life and we must learn to accept it. The deaths of others affect our lives up to the very moment of our own. Our lives can be richer if we accept death as a fact, not a taboo.

Since every death diminishes us a little, we grieve—not so much for the death as for ourselves. And the widow's grief is the sharpest of all, because she has lost the most. But few people understand that grief can represent emotional growth, an enrichment of the self. It is cruel that women are not educated in the progress of grief, since so many of us face the absolutely inevitable prospect of widowhood. Other cultures, other ages laid down protocols of behavior which, no matter how rigid they may seem to us, were at least a guideline for widows to grasp as they suffered through the various stages of grief. But today, widows have little to guide them. The various efforts to help bereaved women—widow-to-widow services, funeral home booklets, efforts of banks and brokerage houses looking for "widow's mite" accounts, even the courses in death now offered by some universities and colleges—are nothing but a Hansel and Gretel trail of bread crumbs. They are no guide to grief. Society's distaste for death is so great that widows tend to become invisible women. They are disturbing reminders of mortality and grief. Yet we are all mortal. And grief is a healing process, not a disease.

If only someone whom I respected had sat me down after Martin died and said, "Now, Lynn, bereavement is a wound. It's like being very, very badly hurt. But you are healthy. You are strong. You will recover. But recovery will be slow. You will grieve and that is painful. And your grief will have many stages, but all of them will be healing."

From Widow

Solitude

Voices

LONELY TIMES

It's mostly when I have a relationship with somebody and it ends. That leaves a big space.

Sally A., age 33

Even on my wedding anniversary I wasn't particularly lonely. I've heard other widows say, "Oh, this week is my wedding anniversary and I'm so alone." I don't feel that way. It was an anniversary when he was with me. Once he was gone, that date became meaningless.

Adele F., married 30 years,
widowed 1 year, age 59

Weekends really panic me right now. I can sort of go through weekdays O.K. but I need to make sure I'm doing something to fill up every weekend. Those are the times my former partner is free from work and I don't want to be wishing that I was doing something with her. So I have to be doing something with somebody else.

Jesse F., age 34

Holidays don't bother me in the least. I've been alone on a lot of them. I've been alone on Christmas a number of times. I've always felt like it should bother me, but it never has. I don't do anything different from an ordinary day. I don't buy myself a present. Nothing. Same with birthdays. In the past ten years I've been alone on my birthday more often than with someone. Dates, anniversaries, holidays—they just don't have

any meaning for me at all.

But, for some strange reason, Sundays sometimes get to me at night. I don't know why that is. It's about the only time that I'll feel a little funny being alone. I'll usually go out and take a long walk.

Patrick R., married 4 years,
divorced 2 years, age 34

Once in a while I get lonely. But I'm at the point where I don't have very many emotions so I say, "Thank goodness I'm feeling lonely. It's good to have some kind of feeling." It's a little negative and a little sad but it's O.K. It isn't at all powerful. It's perfectly fine with me. I think I was maybe more lonely when I was married.

Ellen B., married 22 years,
divorced 3 years, age 58

When the children are away on weekends with their mother, I really miss them. I'm less lonely when they're with me. When they're at home I don't often wish the company of another adult. But I do sometimes when they're gone.

Bruce F., married 10 years,
separated 2 years, age 38

I took some hard medical tests. I don't know how much blood they took out of my arm. They did all kinds of things that made me feel awful. I got back to my apartment and it was the first time I didn't have anybody to complain to. To tell how awful I felt.

Eleanor M., married 32 years,
widowed 10 years, age 73

Holidays affect me. I'm sure that everybody who is single probably has an experience about holidays. This is the roughest time for me, particularly because my parents are dead, my brother and I are not terribly close, and the rest of my family and I have nothing to do with each other. So, at holiday time, when I'm bombarded with the message "This is family hour," I really feel my uniqueness as a single person, and it's not a positive uniqueness.

Holidays are a time of great expectation.

They're people-centered. They're party-centered. And if you're a person who spends time alone a lot, the only thing the holidays do is call into question your state.

Donna R., married 2 years,
divorced 7 years, age 30

It's when I'm feeling a lack of self-confidence. Or it's when I feel really excited about something and I don't want to tell one of my girl friends. I'd like there to be somebody to ask me what I did tonight so I could tell them about this exciting thing.

Cindy W., age 24

COPING WITH LONELINESS

The feeling of loneliness often comes with fatigue. If I'm tired and lonely I'll go to sleep. Often I wake up feeling better. If I don't I will force myself to go out alone. I'll say, "Damn it, do it! Go out. Where would you like to go? What do you want to do?" If I can't pull that off for some reason, I may drink alone. As a last resort I'll turn on the television, but that usually is no solution.

George P., age 25

When I feel lonely I call a friend. I never tell them that I'm lonely, but they know. They can hear my voice. We'll talk about it. I mean, we consider it a tragedy, a reality, part of the plight of life.

Mark B., age 28

When I feel lonely I'll play my records. Or read. Sometimes I have a high-ball.

Eleanor M., married 32 years,
widowed 10 years, age 73

When I'm feeling lonely I just get outside and do something athletic. A lot of times I'll walk or ride my bike. But there is no magic thing I do that makes me feel less lonely.

Donna R., married 2 years,
divorced 7 years, age 30

I've had maybe a total of two minutes of loneliness in the last year. I just look at it and say, "Goodbye, forget it." Because of my religious training I'm now able to erase the mind-set that leads to feeling lonely. I still am aware that I am alone, but I don't have to feel sad about it.

Also, I have very close friends who are part of my religious community. I know that I can call on them. I can have fun with them any time I want to. There's no uncertainty in that at all. It works the same way for me as for the early Puritan communities. I doubt that the Puritans got lonely very much.

Before I got into the community and learned to deal with loneliness, I spent a lot of time walking the streets alone. I'd walk and look at things and sort of feel a beautiful sadness about the whole thing. It was almost gratifying.

Max F., age 29

I get lonely in November when the days are short, especially the time between five and eight in the evening. I start a fire and try to make it cozy because the cold and dreariness make me feel very lonely.

Jennifer F., married 5 years,
divorced 5 years, age 34

Sometimes when you come home from work it's just so still, it's getting dark, and you walk in and there's nobody there. You've got to do something. So you turn on the records. I think that's why I'm such a phone freak. That's what I do most often when I have that feeling. I have a huge phone bill. I call my friends all over the country. That's how I fill up the void.

Sara C., age 31

I feel loneliest when I go to bed. I have a friend who feels the same way. In fact, she used to take her child's teddy bear to bed with her. Sometimes she'd take her child to bed with her so she wouldn't have to sleep alone. I thought about that too. I have my daughter's teddy bears here and I'm tempted to take one to bed with me.

Jesse F., age 34

ENJOYING SOLITUDE

Reading, jogging, listening to records—these are all activities which allow me to sort out and think about who I am, apart from and in relation to others. I write poetry and short pieces and need privacy for this as well.

Michael B., age 30

I've gotten used to doing things myself. I'm sort of a private person. I don't have to be with somebody all the time. I'd rather have my coffee and read the morning paper all by myself than go with a bunch of people.

Eleanor M., married 32 years,
widowed 10 years, age 73

Solitude is a time to think about who you are, where you are, where you're going. I'll ask myself, "O.K., is where I am pretty good or do I want to make some changes? What do I want to do?" I'm one of these people who sits down and makes lists of things. I weigh things very carefully. It seems to be a rejuvenating process for me.

Patrick R., married 4 years,
divorced 2 years, age 34

I wake up early every morning and I stay in bed for about an hour just thinking. Some-times it's about work; sometimes about the people in my life; sometimes about me. That hour gets me in a good mind-set for the day.

Lisa S., age 30

When I'm home, I'm me, always. And it's the only time I'm really aware of that. With most people I am much more externally oriented. I change a lot depending on who I am with at work or elsewhere. I'm interested in how I change. But I like to come back to me and I can only do that when I'm alone. That's why, after a day at work, it's very nice to be totally by myself. That's one of the most positive things about living by myself.

Donna R., married 2 years,
divorced 7 years, age 30

I like sleeping alone. Sometimes I find that sleeping with others can be a bit unpleasant or uncomfortable when you're really tired. Sleeping alone is great when you really want to get down to the business of resting up.

George P., age 25

Solitude

HENRY DAVID THOREAU

Men frequently say to me, "I should think you would feel lonesome down there, and want to be nearer to folks, rainy and snowy days and nights especially." I am tempted to reply to such,—This whole earth which we inhabit is but a point in space. How far apart, think you, dwell the two most distant inhabitants of yonder star, the breadth of whose disk cannot be appreciated by our instruments? Why should I feel lonely? Is not our planet in the Milky Way? This which you put seems to me not to be the most important question. What sort of space is that which separates a man from his fellows and makes him solitary? I have found that no exertion of the legs can bring two minds much nearer to one another. What do we want most to dwell near to? Not to many men surely, the depot, the post-office, the bar-room, the meeting-house, the school-house, the grocery, Beacon Hill, or the Five Points, where men most congregate, but to the perennial source of our life, whence in all our experience we have found that to issue, as the willow stands near the water and sends out its roots in that direction. This will vary with different natures, but this is the place where a wise man will dig his cellar. . . . I one evening overtook one of my townsmen, who has accumulated what is called "a handsome property,"—though I never got a *fair* view of it,—on the Walden road, driving a pair of cattle to market, who inquired of me how I could bring my mind to give up so many of the comforts of life. I answered that I was very sure I liked it passably well; I was not joking. And so I went home to my bed, and left him to pick his way through the darkness and the mud to Brighton,—or Bright-town,—which place he would reach some time in the morning.

Any prospect of awakening or coming to life to a dead man makes indifferent all times and places. The place where that may occur is always the same, and indescribably pleasant to all our senses. For the most part we allow only outlying and transient circumstances to make our occasions. They are, in fact, the cause of our distraction. Nearest to all things is that power which fashions their being. . . .

We are the subjects of an experiment which is not a little interesting to me. Can we not do without the society of our gossips a little while under these circumstances,—have our own thoughts to cheer us? Confucius says truly, "Virtue does not remain as an abandoned orphan; it must of necessity have neighbors."

With thinking we may be beside ourselves in a sane sense. By a conscious effort of the mind we can stand aloof from actions and their consequences; and all things, good and bad, go by us like a torrent. We are not wholly involved in Nature. I may be either the driftwood in the stream, or Indra in the sky looking down on it. I *may* be affected by a theatrical exhibition; on the other hand, I *may not* be affected by an actual event which appears to concern me more. I only know myself as a human entity; the scene, so to speak, of thoughts and affections; and am sensible of a certain doubleness by which I can stand as remote from myself as from another. However intense my experience, I am conscious of the presence and criticism of a part of me, which, as it were, is not a part of me, but spectator, sharing no experience, but taking note of it; and that is no more I than it is you. When the play, it may be the tragedy, of life is over, the spectator goes his way. It was a kind of fiction, a work of the imagination only, so far as he

I never found the companion that was so companionable as solitude.

was concerned. This doubleness may easily make us poor neighbors and friends sometimes.

I find it wholesome to be alone the greater part of the time. To be in company, even with the best, is soon wearisome and dissipating. I love to be alone. I never found the companion that was so companionable as solitude. We are for the most part more lonely when we go abroad among men than when we stay in our chambers. A man thinking or working is always alone, let him be where he will. Solitude is not measured by the miles of space that intervene between a man and his fellows. The really diligent student in one of the crowded hives of Cambridge College is as solitary as a dervish in the desert. The farmer can work alone in the field or the woods all day, hoeing or chopping, and not feel lonesome, because he is employed; but when he comes home at night he cannot sit down in a room alone, at the mercy of his thoughts, but must be where he can "see the folks," and recreate, and, as he thinks, remunerate himself for his day's solitude; and hence he wonders how the student can sit alone in the house all night and most of the day without ennui and "the blues," but he does not realize that the student, though in the house, is still at work in *his* field, and chopping in *his* woods, as the farmer in his, and in turn seeks the same recreation and society that the latter does, though it may be a more condensed form of it.

Society is commonly too cheap. We meet at very short intervals, not having had time to acquire any new value for each other. We meet at meals three times a day, and give each other a new taste of that old musty cheese that we are. We have had to agree on a certain set of rules, called etiquette and politeness, to make this frequent meeting tolerable and that we need not come to open war. We meet at the post-office, and at the sociable, and about the fireside every night; we live thick and are in each other's way, and stumble over one another, and I think that we thus lose some respect for one another. Certainly less frequency would suffice for all important and hearty communications. Consider the girls in a factory,—never alone, hardly in their dreams. It would be better if there were but one inhabitant to a square mile, as where I live. The value of a man is not in his skin, that we should touch him.

I have a great deal of company in my house; especially in the morning, when nobody calls. Let me suggest a few comparisons, that some one may convey an idea of my situation. I am no more lonely than the loon in the pond that laughs so loud, or than Walden Pond itself. What company has that lonely lake, I pray? And yet it has not the blue devils, but the blue angels in it, in the azure tint of its waters. The sun is alone, except in thick weather, when there sometimes appear to be two, but one is a mock sun. God is alone,—but the devil, he is far from being alone; he sees a great deal of company; he is legion. I am no more lonely than a single mullein or dandelion in a pasture, or a bean leaf, or sorrel, or a horse-fly, or a bumble-bee. I am no more lonely than the Mill Brook, or a weathercock, or the north star, or the south wind, or an April shower, or a January thaw.

From Walden *by Henry David Thoreau*

Books

LONELINESS

by Clark E. Moustakas
Prentice-Hall, Inc., 1961

Clark Moustakas identifies two kinds of loneliness: "The loneliness of modern life may be considered two ways: the existential loneliness which inevitably is a part of human experience, and the loneliness of self-alienation and self-rejection which is not loneliness at all but a vague and disturbing anxiety." It is the former kind of loneliness that Moustakas explores and celebrates in this book.

Existential loneliness is the bone-rattling recognition of the fact that no one else but you can experience fully what you feel, who you are. Thomas Wolfe for one, Moustakas writes, "regarded loneliness as an intrinsic condition of existence:

'The whole condition of my life now rests upon the belief that loneliness, far from being a rare and curious phenomenon, peculiar to myself and a few other solitary men, is the actual and inevitable fact of human existence.' "

The experience and acceptance of this essential loneliness, Moustakas tells us, is central to an integrated, whole personality. And, ironically, those who have fully experienced loneliness often discover themselves not cut off from the rest of the world but of a piece with the entirety of existence. Moustakas offers the testimony of Antoine St. Exupery, Emily Dickinson, and other artists to support his vision of the mystical and unifying powers of the experience of absolute loneliness.

Besides his own thoughts on the subject, the author presents portraits of the loneliness of many other people. Most of us can find ourselves in there somewhere. And whether or not we can finally agree about the creative, unifying powers of loneliness, *Loneliness* remains a touchstone for those who have experienced those awesome, sometimes terrifying moments of universal quiet in which the only sound was a single heart beating.

THE LAST OF THE MOUNTAIN MEN

by Harold Peterson
Charles Scribner's Sons, 1969

Sylvan Hart is his name. He lives alone on the banks of the Middle Fork of the Salmon River (River of No Return), surrounded by a vast Idaho wilderness. He is an avid reader, a superb craftsman, a prospector, a gardener, a hunter. The stuff of his life is more the myth of America's past than the reality of America's present. He is a one-man time warp, dressed in buckskin, shouldering his flintlock rifle.

For nearly 40 years now, Hart has been living his solitary wilderness life. But contrary to what we might expect, his is no spare, grinding existence. He lives amply and artfully. He grows at least 20 kinds of vegetables in his garden; he eats bear, elk, salmon, rabbit, trout, grouse, you name it; he gathers edible wild roots and berries. His handmade clothes of animal hide are gorgeous. He makes jewelry, beautiful copper kitchen utensils, and superbly crafted rifles. He reads Russian literature and studies Greek. And he never "works" more than six hours a day, though it's hard to tell his work from his play.

Unlike Thoreau, Hart isn't living in the wilderness to prove a point. He just likes to live life his own way. It is a simple, if extraordinary, lesson in the joys of self-reliance.

SYLVAN HART

On the River of No Return, in the country whose name, according to legend, is Light on the Mountains, there lives a gray-bearded man who has turned back time. At Five Mile Bar, beyond which no human soul dwells, Jedediah Smith and Christopher Carson have but recently passed by, and the year is 1844 forever.

As a young man, dismayed by the destruction of the final frontiers, Sylvan Hart recanted civilization and marched off into this Idaho fastness armed with a few staples, an ax, a rifle, and a master's degree in engineering. There, in the last wilderness, where one winter's snows might fall into another's before a visitor came, he became the last of the Mountain Men. Soon to be known as Buckskin Bill, he fashioned his own clothes of deerskin. He constructed adobe-covered buildings with hand-hewn timbers. He mined copper, smelted it, refined it, and made utensils. He even made his own flintlock rifles, boring them on an ingenious handmade machine, to "save the bother of store-bought ammunition." To pay for infrequent trips to Burgdorf (pop. 6, in winter 0), where he purchased only powder, books, and Darjeeling tea, he panned gold. . . .

From Hart's former habitation, now little more than a depression, a low pile of stones, and the rusted remains of a stove, one could have seen only a century-old cabin used as a storehouse in pioneer years. Its shredded shakes and long departed chinking merely reinforced an in-pressing sense of solitude produced by the return to elemental earth of Bill's cabin, one of the region's few human dwellings.

"I've got six months, from November on, when this place is just like it's always been," Hart said, reclining on a grassy slope, sprig of grass between his teeth. "Nobody visits, I get mail twice a month. If I want to go anywhere, I put a pack on my back, get my gun, take off, and stay as little or long as I like.

"For the city man, life is just a jumble, like the facts in a college freshman's notebook. But you can ask me anything about nearly anything, and I can answer because I've had time to think about it."

Every word, every copper pot, had been tacit answer to the basic question, the question I had refrained from asking, but now I wanted it direct. "Why," I said as offhandedly as possible, "did you come here in the first place?" Aware of all romantic speculations as to lost loves and bitter misanthropies, but believing none, I knew too that none of Bill's good friends had ever, in all their talking, gotten Bill's answer.

"It is," said Buckskin slowly but readily, "a custom of my family, going back about three hundred years, for the young men to stay in the woods for at least a year. The first John Hart, who came here in 1635, did it, moving from England to Warhampton in unsettled Bucks County, Pennsylvania. The fourth John Hart, who signed the Declaration of Independence, went to then-wild Staten Island for a while. A succeeding John Hart was one of the first Kansans, and my grandfather went to the Creek country of Oklahoma. I just liked it so well I never came out."

From *The Last of the Mountain Men*

THE FALL

by Albert Camus
Vintage Books, 1956

The Fall tells the story of a man's efforts to construct a self, to orchestrate rather than live his life. A bachelor Parisian lawyer, the protagonist champions the underdog, helps blind people across the street, befriends the down and out, and defends lost causes. He allows, indeed encourages, people to take advantage of his generosity. He is at his happiest and best when helping one poor unfortunate or another.

But one day, in an instant of profound insight, he perceives that his whole life, all his good works, are based not on altruism but on vanity—he wants and needs the applause, or at least the notice, of others. All his kindnesses are quite public, so others are sure to remark what a fine and selfless chap he is. Once he realizes this, he suffers enormously from a sense of guilt. He can no longer abide the good opinion of others, since it underscores his hypocrisy. He now builds a life of depravity, insensitivity, and debauchery, in part, he says, to deaden the pain of his own feelings of guilt.

At last he leaves Paris and his old life, travels, and finally takes up residence in Amsterdam, where he sells legal advice to underworld people and acts as what he calls a "judge penitent" to tell his own guilt and induce others to admit theirs.

The Fall is a highly philosophical morality play about the modern individual and the modern conscience. The book's protagonist is the true existential person—alone in space and time, making his own way, creating his own universe.

GIFT FROM THE SEA

by Anne Morrow Lindbergh
Random House, 1955

Gift from the Sea is a contemplation on the uses of solitude. Though it is addressed particularly to family women, its message about the need for solitude in modern America is pertinent to everyone. It is a poetical meander in the inner world.

Ann Lindbergh's occasion for writing this book was a solitary vacation at the beach. There, alone, reflective, her life enormously simplified, she pondered how the speedy, complicated modern world works its ill inside us all, keeping us from acting upon our own deepest needs—for simplicity, for the integration of inner and outer life.

But in solitude comes the opportunity to slow down, to reflect, to gain a deeper vision of ourselves, our responsibilities, and our needs. "Every person," Lindbergh writes, "should be alone sometime during the year, some part of each week and each day." It is normally less difficult, of course, for single people to get that solitude; but often no less difficult for them to use it well. Lindbergh says solitude should help teach us simplicity. With simplicity come fewer distractions; clarity is possible; the spirit comes into focus.

There are no self-improvement exercises here for achieving simplicity and integration. But Lindbergh's gentle touch may help guide the reader in the right direction.

JOURNAL OF A SOLITUDE

by May Sarton
W.W. Norton & Company, Inc., 1973

May Sarton intended this journal to be a way into her deeper self: "Now I hope to break through into the rough, rocky depths, to the matrix itself. There is violence there and anger never resolved. My need to be alone is balanced against my fear of what will happen when suddenly I enter the huge empty silence if I cannot find support there."

Whether she succeeded on her own terms, for herself, we can never really know. But for the reader of *Journal of a Solitude*, Sarton succeeds marvelously in revealing the life of a self turning inward and turning outward and always, no matter the visitors, no matter even the good and close friends, always alone.

This isn't one of those narcissistic confessional journals, so toweringly vain and sentimental. Sarton isn't an exhibitionist; she is a kind of scientist of the soul, exposing herself to her own rigorous, highly intelligent scrutiny.

The pages of this journal record Sarton making her way through a year—from September to September—mostly in her small-town New Hampshire home, occasionally off somewhere to give readings or lectures or visit with friends. It is a year, like most years for most of us, of personal and professional struggle—some wins, some losses, some draws, and at the end, maybe, we stand a few inches beyond where we were before.

THE SILENT LIFE
by Thomas Merton
Farrar, Straus and Giroux, 1957

Living at the furthest extreme of the unmarried, unpaired state are those who choose a monastic way of life. This beautiful book by Thomas Merton is at once a meditation upon and an explanation of the monastic way.

As Merton expresses it, in the austerity, the solitude, and the silence of this life one sees through to the very bottom of existence and thereby becomes one with God. The aim in leaving society seems to be to remove oneself from the situation in which the human ego is the dominant structure, and to enter a situation in which the ego is meant to, helped to, dissolve.

Merton gives a brief history of various Western monastic traditions, among them the Clunaic, the Cistercian, the Carthusian, the Camaldolese. Camaldolese monks are hermits who have no contact with society and only a very little with each other. And some choose to become even more removed. Merton writes, "After five years of solemn profession, a hermit who is well qualified and tested may receive permission to live absolutely alone and undisturbed in his cell, never coming out to join the others . . . except three times a year . . . ." The singular advantage of such austere monasticism is that it makes it possible for a pure contemplative life of real solitude and simplicity.

Some examine solitude down to the very bone and see the anguished face of the isolated self. Others, like Merton, look and see the human personality doing its most exalted work. Without prescribing the monastic way, Merton teaches much about solitude.

ROBINSON CRUSOE
by Daniel Defoe
E.P. Dutton & Co., Inc., 1972

Robinson Crusoe has worked his way into our collective psyche—he is the archetypal solitary man. Defoe's classic novel isn't just a good children's adventure story, it's an excellently mapped journey over the terrain of solitude.

Robinson Crusoe sets out adventuring at an early age, against his father's wishes. Before the shipwreck that tosses him onto his island, he gets a hefty dose of experience under his belt—among other things, he's enslaved by pirates for a couple of years, and after his escape he becomes a plantation owner in Brazil. Then, his thirst for excitement not yet slaked, he embarks on that fatal sea voyage. A storm sinks the ship; he alone survives and makes his way to the tropical island that is to be his home for 24 years.

The details of his day-to-day life make for wonderful reading—how he makes his clothes, builds his shelter, gathers, hunts, and prepares food, protects himself from "savages." There is also the continuing drama of his loneliness, his bitterness, his growing religious faith, his fundamental toughness and determination, his overwhelming patience. We're with him. By the time Friday arrives on the scene, our hearts leap and flutter as his does, to have companionship after all those years alone. There's much in this fine old book worth meeting up with and mulling over.

Work

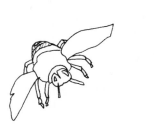

Voices

ON THE JOB

I need a lot of pats on the back and that's why I'm glad that I have my job. If I didn't have it I wouldn't be getting praise from anything else.

Cindy W., age 24

Work is tied up with my whole identity and my success in living. It's central to my feeling of independence. It lets me know I can take care of myself and can manage this whole life. A lot of it is having enough money so that I can reciprocate—give presents and be fluid. And it's also important that I'm surrounded by people who like me.

Sara C., age 31

Becoming single has made me more aware of myself and therefore more aware of what I'm doing at work and how effective I am there. In a sense it's made me more conscientious. I'm willing to put more quality into it. I enjoy my work more.

Bruce F., married 10 years,
separated 2 years, age 38

I've chosen to have freedom to do the artistic work that I want to do and live with less money. I could get a lot of money if I wanted to work in an office. I could have loads of stuff.

I don't have free time as such. All days are pretty much the same to me. I don't distinguish between weekdays and weekends. There seems to be endless stuff to do. I suppose free time is when you're not working.

When I'm at home I'm usually working. But even when I go out, when I'm out walking around, I'm looking at things that I might include in my pictures.

Mark B., age 28

I find that most of the women in my business are single and most of the men are married. So aside from the whole thing about male/female roles, there's also a very strong dynamic of married/single going on. For instance, I often would like to have dinner with one of the other men in the office to discuss work, ideas, etc. But that's usually out of the question. Two men have told me that they'd love to have dinner, but their wives wouldn't understand. I said, "Would it be different if I were married?" and they said, "Yes."

Lisa S., age 30

The structure is what makes it important. It's a social structure as well as a growing structure. Usually I have jobs that make me feel good as a person. Given my lack of people outside of work, I would not be able to stand a job where I didn't feel people respected me. The social thing goes up and down but work is something I can always count on. It's always there, like a friend. My other life is a lot less predictable.

Donna R., married 2 years,
divorced 7 years, age 30

I do housecleaning for a friend. I do it for Social Security so that I'll get Medicare when I'm 62. You can do housework and earn $50

a quarter and get points for Social Security that way. Some people might consider housecleaning low status, but it isn't as far as I'm concerned. In Zen practice, menial labor is a very desirable way to pass your time.

Ellen B., married 22 years,
divorced 3 years, age 58

Work offers me money, prestige, self-satisfaction, friendships, travel opportunities, social situations. It has always been very fulfilling and challenging, a learning process.

It seems to me that attitudes toward work are different for a single person with no dependents compared to those of someone with a family to support. There isn't that desperate need to "hold on" and the constant fear of being fired. You can try something entirely new, making great financial sacrifices, since you're the only one who's involved.

Sometimes I really dread growing old alone. But I am saving money to open my own business so that I can always be busy—no retirement at 65. I know a number of women who have grown old beautifully by themselves by keeping constantly busy, learning new things, traveling, and never feeling old.

Ruth G., age 46

I do all kinds of volunteer work for the hospital, family services, and other groups. I'm just a compulsive have-to-work person. I was raised that way, that you do your share in life. Maybe that's my religious training. I know I'd miss it. I can see by looking at the widowers here that forced retirement is a terrible thing. Many of the men just don't know what to do with themselves.

Eleanor M., married 32 years,
widowed 10 years, age 73

Being single in some ways makes my work harder for me. I'm a writer, which means that my work time is spent alone. Most people interact with others on the job. Take meetings. Nothing ever gets done in a meeting. I think meetings are mainly so people can have some social interaction. But there's no interaction with my work. So it's really important for me to plan to be with others when I'm not working.

Jesse F., age 34

MONEY

I can live on $2000 a year quite comfortably. I realize most other people can't. I pay $80 a month for my room, so that's nearly $1000 a year for living space. I never eat out. I'll go out with my family or if someone else wants to treat me. That's fine, as long as I don't feel like a leech. I buy my own food very economically so I can keep it down to $60 a month, about $700 a year. I do my own car repairs. I hardly ever buy clothes. I get some

for Christmas. I've got wealthy parents so they usually come through. I buy used books. For entertainment, sometimes I'll go to movies. It's not an expensive life—I could spend twice as much, obviously. That would be tremendous. I could eat cashews instead of peanuts. But no problem. I learned to live cheaply when I was in VISTA. I earned about $3500 in a little over a year and came back with more than $1000. I learned how to do it. It's really easy. You can eat well—you don't have to eat potatoes.

My father thinks I should be making $20,000 a year or more. And no question, I could. I was making pretty good money as a computer programmer until I gave it up to try writing. But I have skills. It's just that I don't want to do certain things just to make money.

Max F., age 29

I don't have a life insurance policy because I don't have anyone to worry about. I do have a long-term disability policy, because if I get ill and can't work there is no one to take care of me financially. I spend money freely since I don't need to save for any children's education or a spouse's well-being.

Ruth G., age 46

I don't have a large income but it allows me to live comfortably. In terms of what I do, where I go, how I entertain, what I wear, I'm frugal. I have to be. If I had more money I'd travel more. I'd live more decadently.

George P., age 25

I've been healthy as hell since I've been on my own. I can't afford to get sick. I stopped carrying health insurance. I don't have any cushion money. And I'm doing that on purpose. I want to see how far I can walk on the edge. I want to be able to say, "Whatever happens to me is going to be good from here on out. I can handle whatever comes down." One time I got down to seventy cents in the world. I had stopped working and I had quit

paying my bills. I said to myself, "O.K., you've got seventy cents in your pocket. Your credit is zilch. What are you going to do?" I hitchhiked for the weekend. And came back with seventy cents and after that I said, "Well, hell, you know you can get by. You know you'll be O.K. Now, you can get back to work."

Larry H., married 4 years,
separated 2 years, age 32

I'm not interested in making a heck of a lot of money. I'm not interested in owning anything. Money to me is just a source of security, having enough so that if I don't like what I'm doing I can say, "I don't like this. I'm going off to do something else." It mainly is to buy me the power to control my own destiny.

Patrick R., married 4 years,
divorced 2 years, age 34

My Routine

MAY SARTON

I knew, from having watched my father hack down the incredible amount of work he accomplished day by day and year by year, how supportive a routine is, how the spirit moves around freely in it as it does in a plain New England church. Routine is not a prison, but the way into freedom from time. The apparently measured time has immeasureable space within it, and in this it resembles music.

The routine I established in the first ten days has remained much the same. It revolves around the early morning hours at my desk, then moves gradually out into the rest of the house, as I lie down after lunch in the cosy room for an hour or two, and finally get up and, from May through November, go outdoors to garden for two or three hours before supper. In winter there are always indoor games to be played, such as doing a laundry or getting the files in order (a job that is never done!) or writing letters. I find that I must get up early, at six in summer, at half past six in winter when the morning star is still bright in the dark sky, or the best hours of the day get crowded in. I have to go to bed early if I am to have primary energy to call on for the morning's work.

I found out very soon that the house demanded certain things of me. Because the very shape of the windows has such good proportions, because the builder cared about form, because of all I brought with me, the house demands that everywhere the eye falls it falls on order and beauty. So, for instance, I discovered in the first days that it would be necessary to keep the kitchen counter free of dirty dishes, and that means washing up after each meal; that the big room is so glorious, and anyone in the house is so apt to go to the kitchen windows to look out at the garden or into the sunset, that it would be a shame to leave it cluttered up. The white walls are a marvelous background for flowers, and from the beginning I have considered flowers a necessity, quite as necessary as food. So from spring to late October I spend the hour just after breakfast in the garden, picking whatever I need to rearrange or start fresh six or more bunches. It is one of the best hours of the day, unless I am seriously tired; then it becomes, I must confess, a bit of an ordeal. But it is worth it even then, for wherever I look for the rest of the day there is always somewhere a shaft of light on flowers, and I feel them strongly as part of the whole *presence* of the house.

Choosing, defining, creating harmony, bringing that clarity and shape that is rest and light out of disorder and confusion—the work that I do at my desk is not unlike arranging flowers. Only it is much harder to get started on writing something! Teaching also is hard work, and probably (though in a different way) as creative as writing is, but there is always the class there to draw the best out of a teacher, so he does not have to make the same huge effort to "connect with" the work at hand. The writer, at his desk alone, must create his own momentum, draw the enthusiasm up out of his own substance, not just once, when he may feel inspired, but day after day when he often does not. The teacher is supported also by what he teaches, whereas the writer faces a daily battle with self-questioning, self-doubt, and conflict about his own work. Half the time what he finds on his desk in the morning looks hardly worth tinkering with; in the cool morning light every weakness is exposed.

The work that I do at my desk is not unlike arranging flowers. Only it is much harder to get started on writing something.

Every writer has his own ways of getting started, from sharpening pencils to reading the Bible, to pacing the floor. I often rinse out my mind by reading something, and I sometimes manage to put off getting down to the hard struggle for an unconscionable time. Mostly I am helped through the barrier by music. I play records while I am writing, and especially at the start of each day one particular record that accompanies the poem or chapter I am working at. During these last weeks it has been a record by Albinoni for strings and organ. I do not always play that key record, but it is there to draw on—the key to a certain piece of work, the key to that mood. The romantic composers, much as I enjoy listening to them at other times, are no help. Bach, Mozart, Vivaldi—they are what I need—clarity and structure.

Here again the house itself helps. From where I sit at my desk I look through the front hall, with just a glimpse of staircase and white newel post, and through the warm colors of an Oriental rug on the floor of the cosy room, to the long window at the end that frames distant trees and sky from under the porch roof where I have hung a feeder for woodpeckers and nuthatches. This sequence pleases my eye and draws it out in a kind of geometric progression to open space. Indeed, it is just the way rooms open into each other that is one of the charms of the house, a seduction that can only be felt when one is alone here. People often imagine that I must be lonely. How can I explain? I want to say, "Oh no! You see the house is with me." And it is with me in this particular way, as both a demand and a support, only when I am alone here.

By eleven each morning it is time for a cup of coffee and to go out and taste the air, and to see what there may be to harvest from the mailbox on the green. The mail holds me by a thousand threads to all my lives in Europe and scattered over the United States. It reassures me that within the physical solitude of Nelson I am never alone in the world, and I can still hear all the voices and try to answer them, from the great world griefs—starvation in India, apartheid in South Africa, the plight of our own sharecroppers, the agony of the American Negro—to all the more personal joys and conflicts that fly through the air to reach this silent village. Of course I should have the strength of mind to wait till afternoon before I let all these reverberations begin. But that is a self-discipline I have not achieved. Life conspires against art (and maybe a good thing it does!). Without the daily mail I would become less than human. But even here the battle for time to work, and for the quiet state of mind that makes work possible, goes on day after day. I give myself an A on the rare morning when I am so absorbed that I do not lift my head and catch sight of the station wagon bearing the mail, as it flashes past.

In that first week, I felt I was running all the time. There were hundreds of things I had in mind to do, things about the house, things about the garden, besides the spate of poems that had been pushing their way out. But I imagined that, as time went on, this state of affairs would calm down and I myself would calm down, to lead the meditative life, the life of a Chinese philosopher, that my friends quite naturally imagine I must lead here, way off alone in a tiny village, with few interruptions and almost no responsibilities.

From *Plant Dreaming Deep* by May Sarton

Books

WHAT COLOR IS YOUR PARACHUTE?

by Richard Bolles
Ten Speed Press, 1974

The messages of this book are: Don't go looking for work hat-in-hand, and don't settle for a job that you really don't want.

Richard Bolles suggests we stop considering ourselves victims of personnel directors' caprices and start perceiving that we have a lot of control over the kinds of jobs we can get. To achieve this state of mind, the job hunter must do three things:

"Key No. 1: You must decide just exactly what you want to do.

Key No. 2: You must decide just exactly where you want to do it, through your own research and personal survey.

Key No. 3: You must research the organizations that interest you at great length, and then approach the one individual in each organization who has the power to hire you for the job you want."

The book goes on to explain in detail just how to identify your wants, your skills, the appropriate organizations; how to prepare the right kind of résumé; how to present yourself; and how to carry out any number of other job-seeking tasks. It debunks the want-ad approach and most employment agencies. But for those who want to use an agency, it provides a good shoppers' guide. There are statistics and resources and even some exercises to help the job seeker prepare for the hunt.

Particularly useful for people who are looking to change careers after a long time in one field, *What Color Is Your Parachute?* is a thoroughly upbeat and practical book.

WORKING

by Studs Terkel
Avon Books, 1975

The theme of the alienated worker in industrial society goes back at least as far as the Luddites, who perceived the spiritual dangers of industrialization in England and responded by smashing all the "labor saving" machines they could get near. Charlie Chaplin, in his film *Modern Times*, spoke as eloquently as anyone ever has about the worker cut off from the deeper satisfactions of work. Now we have Studs Terkel, an empathetic journalist asking the modern worker, from stewardess to truck driver, from lawyer to receptionist, to "talk about what they do all day and how they feel about what they do."

Mostly how they feel is downright rotten. Very few of the people interviewed for *Working* like their work. What seems to be missing is "meaning," "connection," a sense that what they're doing is an expression of or an extension of themselves. Terkel found this true not only of blue-collar workers and service workers, but of white-collar workers as well.

It would be surprising if many, many readers didn't find some measure of identification with what the author calls the "unquiet desperation" of the American worker. Terkel didn't set out to find unhappy workers so that he could write a diatribe on working conditions. But that's what he found. It seems safe to assume that the "dis-ease" he discovered runs broad and deep. *Working* won't cheer you up, but it may educate you about the grittier realities of the work place.

PRACTICAL EXERCISE NO. 9

Spend as much time as necessary writing an article entitled "Before I die, I want to . . . ." (Things you would like to do, before you die.) Confess them now, and maybe they'll happen.

Or you may prefer to write the article on a similar topic: "On the last day of my life, what must I have done or been so that my life will have been satisfying to me?" When it is finished, go back over it and make two lists: Things Already Accomplished, Things Yet To Be Accomplished. Then make a third column, beside the one called Things Yet To Be Accomplished, listing the particular *steps* that you will have to take, in order to accomplish these things that you have listed.

As you get involved with these exercises you may notice that it is impossible to keep your focus only on your vocation, occupation, career or whatever you call it. You will find some dreams of places you want to visit creeping in, some experiences you want to have, that are not on-the-job, etc. *Don't omit these.* Be just as specific as possible.

Incidentally, you don't have to do the above exercise just once and for all. Some experts in career and life planning suggest making the previous exercise into a continuous one, with a list posted on your office or kitchen wall—crossing out items as you accomplish them, or do them, and adding new ones as they occur to you from month to month.

Turning from dreams (albeit, concrete, solid dreams) to visions, let us talk of goals and purposes—for these are the visions of the future which cause men and women to set their hands to present tasks. Here is an exercise to deal with the goals that drive you (and there always are such, however undefined):

PRACTICAL EXERCISE NO. 10

Think of some practical concrete task or project in your life (hopefully in the present) that you are a) doing successfully and b) enjoying immensely. (Well, besides that!) It could be at work, at school, or in your spare time. But it must be one which really "turns you on." Put down this task in the center of a blank piece of 8½ × 11 paper turned on its side, then take the following steps:

1. Begin at the lower left hand side of the page, and write the word "why?" (do/ did you want to do this), and on the line above it, indented, write that reason, goal, or purpose.

2. Then write "why?" after this answer, too; and on the line above *it*, indented even more, see if you can write an even more basic reason, goal or purpose.

3. Then write "why?" after it, and on the line above . . . etc. Continue this exercise up the paper, until you think you have reached a basic purpose or goal, that is rather ultimate. (You cannot think of any "why?" behind it.)

4. Now, take that most basic goal (the topmost one on the paper), and draw an arrow from it, down to the part of the paper that is beside the "task" with which you began. There write the words "how else?", and think of what other tasks or projects would accomplish the same ultimate goal (the topmost one on your paper).

From *What Color Is Your Parachute!*

177

BORROWING

THE RIGHT REASONS FOR BORROWING

Regardless of whether you are equally convinced at this point, for the moment assume you agree that borrowing money is right for you if your reasons are right.

What might those reasons be?

(1) You are establishing a household or beginning to have a family. Either of these major events in life will take a lot of money—and it's in these, your early years, that you should learn how to use credit wisely and to the best advantage for yourself.

(2) You must make some major purchases. Few Americans can buy a car out of cash on hand and few can buy furniture or appliances that way either. These big-ticket items are traditionally bought with credit. As for a house, virtually all of us borrow to finance that key purchase.

(3) You are faced with a genuine emergency and have not as yet had the opportunity to accumulate a sufficient emergency cash fund. Borrowing to meet emergencies is about as valid a reason as there can be.

(4) There are attractive seasonal sales or specials on which you can save money if you can use a charge account or a time-payment plan or get a low-cost loan from a financial institution. This assumes that the items on sale are ones you really want or need.

(5) You need money for college or other education expenses. This also is a top-notch reason for borrowing either by the student or by the parents. In fact, borrowing for college is the normal thing in America in this era.

THE WRONG REASONS FOR BORROWING

(1) You haven't a reasonable prospect of repaying the loan but you are going ahead anyway and borrowing because you need the money or want the goods or services. Or you are borrowing to the very hilt of your capacity to repay, which means that even a minor miscalculation on your part could force you to default.

(2) You are buying something impulsively and are primarily attracted to the purchase, not because the product is of good quality and reasonably priced, but because the payment terms seem so easy and you are offered a long time to pay up. This is self-deception of the most dangerous kind from your personal financial point of view.

(3) You are charging purchases solely to boost your morale. Some individuals try to beat the blues with an extravagant shopping spree. Doing this on credit can bring on an even bigger attack of melancholy when the bills—with interest—finally come due.

(4) You are using credit to increase your status. Charging a purchase does allow you to pay for things while you're enjoying them. But credit alone can't raise your standard of living.

(5) You are overusing credit generally and failing to maintain an adequate cash reserve. People who do this also tend to live hand to mouth with their cash. They build up little or no savings fund to use during medical or other emergencies. So even if they are able to repay regular debts on schedule, any unexpected financial reversal can be their complete undoing. . .

From Sylvia Porter's Money Book

SYLVIA PORTER'S MONEY BOOK

by Sylvia Porter
Avon Books, 1976

It's always a little unnerving paying money to find out how to handle money. There's that nagging suspicion that only the author of the book will come out ahead. But *Sylvia Porter's Money Book* really is worth the price to those of us who are financial primitives stumbling around in the supercomplexities of modern economics. In this eminently usable encyclopedic guide to spending and saving, Porter provides some economic sophistication and a good introduction to money management.

This practical book steers the reader all over the financial map: personal money management, varieties of bank accounts, loan shopping, buying everything from homes to tires, saving on groceries, clothes, and vacations, making wills, investing, speculating, and more.

The book is excellently organized, so you can find what you need quickly. It is clearly written in straightforward language—no economic jargon—and concepts and procedures are broken down to their fundamentals. In short, it's an invaluable resource book for those working to make do.

THE JOY OF MONEY

by Paula Nelson
Bantam Books, 1975

The Joy of Money is a kind of financial assertiveness-training manual. Aimed particularly at women but in fact appropriate for people of either sex, the book makes a vigorous pitch for financial independence through intelligent and aggressive money management.

First off, Paula Nelson deflates the "Women and Money Mystique," urging women to take charge of their financial affairs. Once you've declared your independence and are steadfastly resolved to become well-off if not downright rich, you must set financial goals for yourself, keeping in mind your abilities and talents that will help you realize the goals. If

you're in debt, of course, your first move must be to get up and out of it. When you're really ready to get going, choose your helpers wisely—banker, lawyer, accountant, insurance agent, real estate broker, stockbroker. You might want to start your own business. If so, make careful plans. If you choose to work for someone else, learn how to negotiate the best possible deal for yourself.

When all that money starts pouring in, you'll need to know a great deal about wise investing—bonds, tax shelters, preferred and common stocks, insurance, gold, art objects, jewelry, and more. And of course you'll need to know how to develop a pleasant relationship with your friend the tax collector.

While not a detailed study of all these matters, *The Joy of Money* is a fairly thorough primer that succeeds in making it seem you needn't be a wizard to do rather well with money.

UP YOUR OWN ORGANIZATION

by Donald M. Dible
The Entrepreneur Press, 1971

If there were a popularity contest for dreams, starting your own business would be a perennial winner. Of course making that dream into a reality calls for more than wishful thinking; it usually means a mountain of planning and effort and a blizzard of legal and financial technicalities. If we're really going to do it, we need all the help we can get.

Dible begins with a few case histories, then gets into the meaty part of the matter: Check your personal resources—physical, mental, and financial. Educate yourself with appropriate books, journals, periodicals, school courses, seminars. If you don't already have one, search for a super product at invention expositions, in new-product periodicals, in doctoral dissertations. Develop a formal business plan that structures your company, identifies markets, locates your plant. Capitalize your firm—Dible provides a list of 40 sources of money. And then get down to business.

Before you invest thousands manufacturing a garbage disposal that plays Mozart, you may want to invest a few dollars in this book.

Part III Questions

Questions

BEING SINGLE

1. How does it happen that you are single?

2. Do people ever ask you why you're not married? If so, how do you answer that question?

3. When you were a child, did you ever imagine that you might be single as an adult? Did you know any single people—relatives? teachers? Did you ever think about how they lived?

4. If you have chosen to be single, why did you make that choice?

5. Do you consider your singleness temporary or permanent? Why?

6. How do your friends, relatives, co-workers feel about your being single? Do they ever make positive or negative comments?

COMPANIONSHIP

7. How important are friends to you? What do they give or take from you?

8. Where do you find friends?

9. Does it make a difference to you whether a friend is single as opposed to married? Do you feel a special kinship with singles?

10. Will you invite a couple over, or go out with a couple, making a threesome? Do couples invite you out?

11. Does it affect your relationship with a single friend if he or she enters into a couple relationship?

12. Are most of your friends your age or do their ages vary? Does it matter? Why?

13. Do you value platonic friendships? Do you find them easy or hard to maintain?

14. How do you arrange to be with others? Are church groups, educational classes, special groups like Parents Without Partners important in your social life? Would you ever buy tickets for two as a way of ensuring you'll spend time with someone else?

15. How important is family to you—parents? siblings? cousins?

16. Can you comment on the companionship you get from books, plants, pets, TV?

HOUSEHOLD

17. What kind of living arrangements do you prefer—by yourself? with roommates? Why? What are the advantages and disadvantages? How important is privacy to you?

18. How did you go about finding your present home? If you live with others, how did you make sure you'd be compatible with them?

19. What are your thoughts about renting a house versus buying one? Did you ever have trouble obtaining housing because you are a single person? What did you do?

20. How do you handle house cleaning and repairs? Where do you get help for jobs that are too big for one person? What do you do about chores that you hate?

21. What is your guest policy? Does it affect your life to have one or more guests staying at your house?

22. Has your single status affected the kinds and amounts of furnishings you have bought, or affected the way you have decorated your place?

23. Where do you usually eat—at home? at restaurants? at friends' places? Why?

24. How do you feel about eating alone at a restaurant? What do you do while waiting for your food? What do you do while eating?

25. What kinds of meals do you prepare at home? Do you give much thought to having a balanced diet?

26. What kind of atmosphere do you create when eating at home alone? Do you read or watch TV or concentrate on the food? How do you

feel about eating by yourself at home?

27. What do you do about leftovers—freeze them? throw them away? Do you have ways of avoiding leftovers, for instance, by buying small cans when shopping?

28. Do you ever get into a food fixation where you'll eat the same food night after night? What breaks you out of it?

LOVING

29. How do you find dates? Have you ever used any of the more unusual ways of dating such as placing a classified advertisement or using a computer dating service?

30. What do you like to do on a date? What's your idea of a great evening? If you go out, who pays?

31. What kind of dating relationship do you prefer—having one steady person? lots of different people?

32. Do friends ever fix you up? How do you handle people who want to fix you up without your asking them to? How do blind dates work out?

33. How important is sex in your life? Has this changed over time?

34. Do you seek out long-term or casual sexual relationships? How do you feel about one-night stands?

35. How do you feel about having sex with someone who is married or involved in some form of a couple relationship?

36. What role does masturbation play in your life? How much of a celebration do you make out of it?

PARENTING

37. If you were married, how is parenting different now that you are single? Is it easier? harder?

38. How do your children enhance your life? Do they provide companionship?

39. What difficulties have children caused you—financial? social?

40. What problems did your children have when you became single? How did you deal with these problems?

41. How do you deal with your ex-mate concerning the children? Are there problems over visiting, school, money?

42. If you never had any children before, what are your thoughts about having children by yourself?

RECREATION

43. Do you prefer to spend your free time mainly by yourself or with others? Why?

44. What things do you like to do all by yourself?

45. How do you feel about traveling or vacationing alone? If you prefer to travel with others, how do you find good traveling companions?

46. How do you spend your free time during evenings and weekends? Do you plan your leisure ahead? What on-going projects or hobbies have you available when you don't know what to do ? What games do you play by yourself?

47. Do you ever plan a weekend of complete solitude? What's it like? What do you do?

48. What do you do when you're alone for the holidays or your birthday? Do you ever celebrate such events by yourself? What do you do?

49. Do you ever take alcohol or other drugs by yourself? What's that like?

50. What's the most fun thing you ever did alone?

51. What kind of entertaining do you do?

SELF

52. How do you work at your personal growth? How do you get to know or like yourself better? For instance, have you attended encounter groups?

53. How do you take stock? Do you keep a diary? Do you talk to yourself? What do you talk about?

54. What role do religious or spiritual activities play in your life?

55. What personality traits do you most value in yourself—courage? autonomy? Does being single foster such characteristics?

56. How do you manage when you are ill?

57. Whom do you seek out when you need help? Do you have a network of friends you can always call on?

58. How do you make important decisions? Do you mull things over by yourself? Do you consult with others?

59. How do cycles affect you? Is there a pattern

to your good times and bad times?

60. Do you ever think about growing old alone? What fears or expectations do you have about it? Can you describe any friend or relative who is good at handling aging alone?

SINGLE AGAIN

61. While part of a couple, did you ever fantasize about becoming single? How did such thoughts, fears, or expectations compare with the reality of being single?

62. Did you prepare in any way for becoming single?

63. How did you cope with losing your mate through death or divorce? What kind of help did you seek out? Did you look for models—other widows, widowers, or divorced people? Have you been a model for others?

64. What affect did becoming single have on you financially?

65. What new things did you learn about yourself when you became single again? How have you changed—more self-reliant? more self-aware?

66. What do you miss most about not being part of a couple?

67. What do you like most about being single? What pleasures have you discovered?

68. How did your friends and relatives react to your becoming single? Did your relationships with any people change?

SOLITUDE

69. What situations make you feel lonely?

70. Are there certain times—of the day, week, year—when you feel lonely?

71. What do you do when you feel lonely—call a friend? turn on the TV?

72. In what ways do you enjoy solitude?

WORK

73. How important a part of your life is your work? Why is it important? What do you get out of your work—friendships? travel opportunities? a sense of who you are?

74. How has being single proved to be an advantage or a disadvantage in terms of your work life?

75. How does the amount of money you have affect the way you live?

76. How would you live differently if you had a lot more money?

77. How do you feel about giving or receiving alimony? If you receive alimony, does that affect your sense of independence?